BAPTISTWAY ADULT BIBLE STUDY GUIDE

Participating in God's Mission

JEFF RAINES
ROBERT SHIPPEY
WILLIAM TINSLEY

BAPTISTWAYPRESS®

Dallas, Texas

Participating in God's Mission—BaptistWay Adult Bible Study Guide

Copyright © 2009 by BAPTISTWAY PRESS®.
All rights reserved.
Printed in the United States of America.

No part of this book may be used or reproduced in any manner whatsoever without written permission except in the case of brief quotations. For information, contact BAPTISTWAY PRESS, Baptist General Convention of Texas, 333 North Washington, Dallas, TX 75246–1798.

BAPTISTWAY PRESS® is registered in U.S. Patent and Trademark Office.

Scripture marked NASB is taken from the 1995 update of the New American Standard Bible®, Copyright © The Lockman Foundation 1960, 1962, 1963, 1968, 1971, 1972, 1973, 1975, 1977, 1995. Used by permission. Unless otherwise indicated, all Scripture quotations in unit 1, lessons 1–4, and unit 3, lessons 8–13, are from the New American Standard Bible (1995 edition).

Scripture marked NRSV is taken from the New Revised Standard Version Bible, copyright 1989, Division of Christian Education of the National Council of the Churches of Christ in the United States of America. Used by permission. All rights reserved. Unless otherwise indicated, all Scripture quotations in unit 2, lessons 5–7, are from the New Revised Standard Version Bible.

Scripture marked NIV is taken from The Holy Bible, New International Version (North American Edition), copyright © 1973, 1978, 1984 by the International Bible Society. Used by permission of Zondervan Publishing House.

BAPTISTWAY PRESS® Management Team
Executive Director, Baptist General Convention of Texas: Randel Everett
Director, Missions, Evangelism, and Ministry Team: Wayne Shuffield
Ministry Team Leader: Phil Miller
Publisher, BAPTISTWAY PRESS®: Ross West

Cover and Interior Design and Production: Desktop Miracles, Inc.
Printing: Data Reproductions Corporation

First edition: June 2009
ISBN-13: 978-1-934731-29-1

How to Make the Best Use of This Issue

Whether you're the teacher or a student—
1. Start early in the week before your class meets.
2. Overview the study. Review the table of contents and read the study introduction. Try to see how each lesson relates to the overall study.
3. Use your Bible to read and consider prayerfully the Scripture passages for the lesson. (You'll see that each writer has chosen a favorite translation for the lessons in this issue. You're free to use the Bible translation you prefer and compare it with the translation chosen for that unit, of course.)
4. After reading all the Scripture passages in your Bible, then read the writer's comments. The comments are intended to be an aid to your study of the Bible.
5. Read the small articles—"sidebars"—in each lesson. They are intended to provide additional, enrichment information and inspiration and to encourage thought and application.
6. Try to answer for yourself the questions included in each lesson. They're intended to encourage further thought and application, and they can also be used in the class session itself.

If you're the teacher—

A. Do all of the things just mentioned, of course. As you begin the study with your class, be sure to find a way to help your class know the date on which each lesson will be studied. You might do this in one or more of the following ways:

- In the first session of the study, briefly overview the study by identifying with your class the date on which each lesson will be studied. Lead your class to write the date in the table of contents on page 7 and on the first page of each lesson.

- Make and post a chart that indicates the date on which each lesson will be studied.
- If all of your class has e-mail, send them an e-mail with the dates the lessons will be studied.
- Provide a bookmark with the lesson dates. You may want to include information about your church and then use the bookmark as an outreach tool, too. A model for a bookmark can be downloaded from www.baptistwaypress.org on the Resources for Adults page.
- Develop a sticker with the lesson dates, and place it on the table of contents or on the back cover.

B. Get a copy of the *Teaching Guide*, a companion piece to this *Study Guide*. The *Teaching Guide* contains additional Bible comments plus two teaching plans. The teaching plans in the *Teaching Guide* are intended to provide practical, easy-to-use teaching suggestions that will work in your class.

C. After you've studied the Bible passage, the lesson comments, and other material, use the teaching suggestions in the *Teaching Guide* to help you develop your plan for leading your class in studying each lesson.

D. You may want to get the additional adult Bible study comments—*Adult Online Bible Commentary*—by Dr. Jim Denison (president, The Center for Informed Faith, Dallas, Texas, and theologian in residence, Baptist General Convention of Texas) that are available at www.baptistwaypress.org and can be downloaded free. An additional teaching plan plus teaching resource items are also available at www.baptistwaypress.org.

E. You also may want to get the enrichment teaching help that is provided on the internet by the *Baptist Standard* at www.baptiststandard.com. (Other class participants may find this information helpful, too.) Call 214-630-4571 to begin your subscription to the printed edition of the *Baptist Standard*.

F. Enjoy leading your class in discovering the meaning of the Scripture passages and in applying these passages to their lives.

Writers of This Study Guide

Jeff Raines, the writer of unit one, lessons one through four, is associate pastor, First Baptist Church, Amarillo, Texas. Dr. Raines is a graduate of Baylor University, Truett Seminary, and Princeton Seminary (D.Min.). He served on the founding board of directors of WorldconneX, and he has also served as the second vice president of the Baptist General Convention of Texas (2008). He and his wife, Darcie, have one son, Mark.

Robert Shippey wrote unit two, lessons five through seven. Dr. Shippey is associate pastor, First Baptist Church, Rome, Georgia. He formerly served on the religion faculty of Shorter College, Rome, Georgia, and also as assistant vice president. He is the author of *Listening in a Loud World*. He holds degrees from Furman University and The Southern Baptist Theological Seminary (Ph.D.).

William (Bill) Tinsley wrote unit three, lessons eight through thirteen. He serves as the leader of WorldconneX, the missions network created by the Baptist General Convention of Texas (see www.worldconnex.org). Prior to this, he served as associate executive director of the Baptist General Convention of Texas; executive director of the Minnesota-Wisconsin Baptist Convention; director of missions in Denton Association, Texas; and pastor for sixteen years.

Participating in God's Mission

How to Make the Best Use of This Issue	3
Writers for This Study Guide	5
Introducing Participating in God's Mission	9

DATE OF STUDY

UNIT ONE
Foundational Truths About God's Mission

6/7 LESSON 1 *Donna* The Mission's Beginning
GENESIS 1:1; ISAIAH 46:5–9; ACTS 17:24–31 15

6/14 LESSON 2 *Donna* The Mission's Motivation
DEUTERONOMY 7:7–8; PSALM 136:1–11, 23–26;
JONAH 3:10—4:3, 9–11; JOHN 3:16;
ROMANS 5:6–8 25

6/21 LESSON 3 *Donna* The Mission's Focus
GENESIS 12:1–3; EXODUS 19:1–6; LUKE 1:46–55 35

6/28 LESSON 4 *Donna* The Mission's Unlimited Reach
GENESIS 12:1–3; ISAIAH 49:5–6; LUKE 2:25–32;
ACTS 1:8; ROMANS 10:12–13 45

UNIT TWO
What God's Mission Is About

7/5 LESSON 5 *Donna* God's Mission: Redemption and Reconciliation
EXODUS 5:22—6:8; 15:1–2, 13; ISAIAH 55:6–7;
COLOSSIANS 1:13–14; HEBREWS 9:11–14 57

7/12 LESSON 6 *Jimmye* God's Mission: Restoration and Justice
DEUTERONOMY 15:1–11; MICAH 6:8;
JEREMIAH 7:1–7; LUKE 4:16–21;
JAMES 1:27; 2:14–16 67

7/19 **LESSON 7** *Jimmye* God's Mission: Embodied in Jesus
   MATTHEW 11:2–6; 23:23–24; JOHN 1:10–14;
   ROMANS 3:21–26; PHILIPPIANS 2:9–11   77

UNIT THREE

God's Call to You

7/26 **LESSON 8** *Jimmye* Experience God's Good News
   LUKE 19:1–10; ACTS 9:1–9, 19B–22; 16:13–15, 25–34   87

8/2 **LESSON 9** *Jimmye* Live in Faithfulness to God
   ROMANS 12   99

8/9 **LESSON 10** *Jimmye* Engage in God's Mission Together
   ACTS 4:32–35; 2 CORINTHIANS 8:1–9;
   1 CORINTHIANS 12:4–13; 1 PETER 2:6–10   109

8/16 **LESSON 11** *Donna* Tell the Good News of Redemption and
   Reconciliation
   2 CORINTHIANS 5:11–21; COLOSSIANS 1:24–29   119

8/23 **LESSON 12** *Donna* Minister to People's Physical Needs
   DEUTERONOMY 10:14–19; AMOS 5:21–24;
   MATTHEW 25:31–46   129

8/30 **LESSON 13** *Donna* Participate in God's Mission to Everyone
   MATTHEW 28:16–20; ACTS 11:19–26;
   REVELATION 5:1–10   137

Our Next New Study   147
Additional Future Adult Bible Studies   149
How to Order More Bible Study Materials   151

Introducing Participating in God's Mission

God's Mission?

What is "God's mission"? The biblical passages in this study can lead you to see that God's mission is much bigger and more comprehensive than you thought. These Scriptures may cause you to ask questions like these: *Is my view of God's mission as big as what God's mission actually is? Do I think of God's mission as only "spiritual"? How important is God's mission? If it's important, what am I doing about it?* This series of studies is intended to help both in offering you greater understanding of God's mission and in encouraging—even challenging—you toward more action in participating in it.

The mission of God may well be the single most important organizing theme of the Bible from Genesis to Revelation.[1] The Bible thus is the story of what God is doing in our world. Therefore, in this series of Bible study lessons, we will trace various aspects of the theme of God's mission—what God is doing—and seek to understand and act on what this means for us.

This Study

The biblical texts selected for this study can be described as *climactic* texts. *Climactic* texts speak in a crucial, pointed manner to a given subject or theme. *Climactic* texts are *foundational* texts. John 3:16 is thus a *climactic* text. The *climactic* texts in this study provide *climactic* insight into the meaning of the mission of God, speaking clearly and powerfully to this theme.

As we study these texts, we will look especially for how they fit together and how they challenge us to understand and act on the fullness of God's mission. Often even people who have been Christians for many years understand and act on only a part of it. This study will seek to examine the full range of God's actions and teachings concerning his mission. It will also challenge us to decide how God is calling us to participate in his mission.

God's Mission and Our Lives

Sometimes people approach Bible study together as merely a social event, without much intent of really learning anything new and certainly not of doing anything about it, at least not beyond what their tradition has taught them. The best group Bible study, though, will challenge our present understanding rather than simply reinforcing what we thought we already knew. Further, it will lead us to action, to changes in behavior.

Perhaps that will happen for you and your class in this study. The study, after all, is about *participating* in God's mission. Consider with your class what you need to do—and what you need to encourage your church to do—truly to participate in God's mission. God has a wonderful plan—his mission—and God invites us to participate in it. How will we respond?

UNIT ONE. FOUNDATIONAL TRUTHS ABOUT GOD'S MISSION

Lesson 1	The Mission's Beginning	Genesis 1:1; Isaiah 46:5–9; Acts 17:24–31
Lesson 2	The Mission's Motivation	Deuteronomy 7:7–8; Psalm 136:1–11, 23–26; Jonah 3:10—4:3, 9–11; John 3:16; Romans 5:6–8
Lesson 3	The Mission's Focus	Genesis 12:1–3; Exodus 19:1–6; Luke 1:46–55
Lesson 4	The Mission's Unlimited Reach	Genesis 12:1–3; Isaiah 49:5–6; Luke 2:25–32; Acts 1:8; Romans 10:12–13

UNIT TWO. WHAT GOD'S MISSION IS ABOUT

| Lesson 5 | God's Mission: Redemption and Reconciliation | Exodus 5:22—6:8; 15:1–2, 13; Isaiah 55:6–7; Colossians 1:13–14; Hebrews 9:11–14 |

Lesson 6	God's Mission: Restoration and Justice	Deuteronomy 15:1–11; Micah 6:8; Jeremiah 7:1–7; Luke 4:16–21; James 1:27; 2:14–16
Lesson 7	God's Mission: Embodied in Jesus	Matthew 11:2–6; 23:23–24; John 1:10–14; Romans 3:21–26; Philippians 2:9–11

UNIT THREE. GOD'S CALL TO YOU

Lesson 8	Experience God's Good News	Luke 19:1–10; Acts 9:1–9, 19b–22; 16:13–15, 25–34
Lesson 9	Live in Faithfulness to God	Romans 12
Lesson 10	Engage in God's Mission Together	Acts 4:32–35; 2 Corinthians 8:1–9; 1 Corinthians 12:4–13; 1 Peter 2:6–10
Lesson 11	Tell the Good News of Redemption and Reconciliation	2 Corinthians 5:11–21; Colossians 1:24–29
Lesson 12	Minister to People's Physical Needs	Deuteronomy 10:14–19; Amos 5:21–24; Matthew 25:31–46
Lesson 13	Participate in God's Mission to Everyone	Matthew 28:16–20; Acts 11:19–26; Revelation 5:1–10

Additional Resources for Studying *Participating in God's Mission*[2]

    Darrell L. Guder and Lois Barrett, ed. *Missional Church: A Vision for the Sending of the Church in North America.* Grand Rapids, Michigan: William B. Eerdmans Publishing Company, 1998.

    Philip Jenkins. *The Next Christendom: The Coming of Global Christianity.* New York: Oxford University Press, 2002.

    Milfred Minatrea. *Shaped by God's Heart: The Passion and Practices of Missional Churches.* San Francisco: Jossey-Bass, 2004.

    Lesslie Newbigin. *The Open Secret: An Introduction to the Theology of Mission.* Revised edition. Grand Rapids, Michigan: William B. Eerdmans Publishing Company, 1995.

    William Tinsley. *Finding God's Vision: Missions and the New Realities.* Rockwall, Texas: Veritas Publishing, 2005.

    Christopher J. H. Wright. *The Mission of God: Unlocking the Bible's Grand Narrative.* Downers Grover, Illinois: IVP Academic, 2006.[3]

NOTES

1. For an extensive treatment by a biblical scholar on this theme, see especially Christopher J. H. Wright, *The Mission of God: Unlocking the Bible's Grand Narrative* (Downers Grover, Illinois: IVP Academic, 2006).
2. Listing a book does not imply full agreement by the writers or BAPTISTWAY PRESS® with all of its comments.
3. The extensive, scholarly treatment of the biblical theme of God's mission in this book is of special significance in understanding the biblical background and direction of this study.

UNIT ONE
Foundational Truths About God's Mission

What is *missions* or *the mission* for the church? Is it a department or division of the church? Is it something carried out somewhere else by *professionals* only? Is it something we practice, talk about, or think about? Is it essential, or is it optional? Over the last 100 to 150 years, Baptists have, in the name of efficiency, outsourced missions to professionals. We have established missions organizations, and missions-minded churches write them checks in order to *do missions*. Individuals become *missions-minded* by learning about or being aware of the work of these professionals.

So what's wrong with this? The problem with this approach is that if we have given our key task to someone else, we may miss what God really has in store for us.

We need to reset our understanding of missions. The words of a great missions scholar might help us in doing this: "Mission is not primarily an activity of the church, but an attribute of God."[1] Instead of viewing missions as something the church elects to do with a percentage of our resources, we need to realize that the mission is God's. God has a mission to our world, and the church is the result of that mission and an instrument in implementing it. Such a shift in thinking affects every aspect of the church's life and of the Christian's life.

These lessons will look at some foundational elements of God's mission and our role in it. Lesson one explores the roots of that mission in God's creating work and dominion over all things. The place the mission begins is with the reality that God is God of all the earth. Lesson two looks at the motivation of God's mission—the love of God. Lesson three moves to God's methods in showing his love to his creation. God calls and creates a people in order that they would show God's love and bear God's message to others. Lesson four explores the universal goal of God's mission. He wants all people to know him.

The texts for these lessons come from various parts of Scripture. God's mission is not confined to the New Testament or to the Great Commission (Matthew 28:19–20). Rather, the entire Bible is a missional book—a result of God's mission with our world. The church is a missional body—the result of God's mission for our world. Truly, our God is a missionary God![2]

UNIT ONE. FOUNDATIONAL TRUTHS ABOUT GOD'S MISSION

Lesson 1	The Mission's Beginning	Genesis 1:1; Isaiah 46:5–9; Acts 17:24–31
Lesson 2	The Mission's Motivation	Deuteronomy 7:7–8; Psalm 136:1–11, 23–26; Jonah 3:10—4:3, 9–11; John 3:16; Romans 5:6–8
Lesson 3	The Mission's Focus	Genesis 12:1–3; Exodus 19:1–6; Luke 1:46–55
Lesson 4	The Mission's Unlimited Reach	Genesis 12:1–3; Isaiah 49:5–6; Luke 2:25–32; Acts 1:8; Romans 10:12–13

NOTES

1. David J. Bosch, *Transforming Mission: Paradigm Shifts in Theology of Mission*, American Society of Missiology Series, No. 16 (Maryknoll, New York: Orbis Books, 1991), 390.
2. Unless otherwise indicated, all Scripture quotations in unit 1, lessons 1–4, are from the New American Standard Bible (1995 edition).

LESSON ONE
The Mission's Beginning

FOCAL TEXTS
Genesis 1:1;
Isaiah 46:5–9; Acts 17:24–31

BACKGROUND
Genesis 1:1;
Isaiah 44:6–28; 46:1–13;
Acts 17:22–31

MAIN IDEA
God's mission begins from the foundation that God's dominion is unlimited.

QUESTION TO EXPLORE
How big is your God?

STUDY AIM
To consider implications and actions that should follow from the biblical truth of God's unlimited dominion

QUICK READ
Our role in God's mission is grounded in proper worship of God alone.

"How great is the Lord," declared the psalmist in an exclamation of praise (Psalm 48:1, New Living Translation). In starting this series of Bible studies, it might be appropriate to turn that declaration into a question for each of us. *How great is the Lord?* How great is your understanding and image of who God is? What is your mental picture of God? In your mind's eye is God more active or more passive? How connected is God to day-to-day affairs here on earth?

Genesis 1:1

In the beginning God created the heavens and the earth.

Isaiah 46:5–9

⁵"To whom would you liken Me
And make Me equal and compare Me,
That we would be alike?
⁶"Those who lavish gold from the purse
And weigh silver on the scale
Hire a goldsmith, and he makes it into a god;
They bow down, indeed they worship it.
⁷"They lift it upon the shoulder and carry it;
They set it in its place and it stands there.
It does not move from its place.
Though one may cry to it, it cannot answer;
It cannot deliver him from his distress.
⁸"Remember this, and be assured;
Recall it to mind, you transgressors.
⁹"Remember the former things long past,
For I am God, and there is no other;
I am God, and there is no one like Me. . . .

Acts 17:24–31

²⁴"The God who made the world and all things in it, since He is Lord of heaven and earth, does not dwell in temples made with hands; ²⁵nor is He served by human hands, as though He needed

anything, since He Himself gives to all people life and breath and all things; ²⁶and He made from one man every nation of mankind to live on all the face of the earth, having determined their appointed times and the boundaries of their habitation, ²⁷that they would seek God, if perhaps they might grope for Him and find Him, though He is not far from each one of us; ²⁸for in Him we live and move and exist, as even some of your own poets have said, 'For we also are His children.' ²⁹"Being then the children of God, we ought not to think that the Divine Nature is like gold or silver or stone, an image formed by the art and thought of man. ³⁰"Therefore having overlooked the times of ignorance, God is now declaring to men that all people everywhere should repent, ³¹because He has fixed a day in which He will judge the world in righteousness through a Man whom He has appointed, having furnished proof to all men by raising Him from the dead."

God's Unlimited Dominion (Genesis 1:1)

If our mission is truly rooted in God's mission, then to get our actions right we must start with our God whose rule is unlimited. The familiar opening phrase of Scripture establishes God's dominion: "In the beginning God created the heavens and the earth" (Genesis 1:1). The creating act of God grounds everything in him—heavens and earth. It also establishes the most fundamental distinction in the universe. God is Creator. All else is creation.

After establishing this unique position of God in the opening phrase, much of the rest of Scripture addresses the struggle of humanity either against this truth or to understand and comprehend it.

Israel's role was to obey and serve this one God of heaven and earth. This task would prove, however, a crucial point of tension in Israel's relationship with neighboring peoples and their local deities. Each group had their own god or gods, and the ancient mindset assumed that conflicts among peoples reflected the relative strength of their gods. In this context, many of the greatest events in Israel's history are part of a learning process. We see this learning process in action as either Israel or Israel's neighbors/oppressors discovered the true God of creation.

How great is our God? As God said to Isaiah, "I am the first and I am the last, and there is no God besides Me.... Is there any God besides Me, or is there any other Rock? I know of none" (Isaiah 44:6, 8).

Since Genesis 3, humanity has struggled to grasp and retain the implications of the greatness of God. We have consistently limited God and revealed a lack of understanding of God's limitless rule and domain. If our God is too small, then we are offering what belongs to God to something or someone else. The name for our attempts to offer what belongs to God to any other person, entity, or thing is idolatry.

Idolatry in the Old Testament (Isaiah 46:5–9)

At its root, idolatry chips away at the distinction between Creator and creation. In the original order of things, humanity was to *worship* God and to serve as a steward in the care and *use* of created things. In idolatry

DO YOU REMEMBER?

Isaiah challenged the exiles, who might have been tempted to idolatry or despair, to "remember" what God had done (Isa. 46:8–9). The call to remember occurs throughout the Old Testament and was a crucial element of following God. For example, when the Israelites crossed the Jordan River, finally entering the Promised Land, Joshua told them to take twelve stones from the river to form an altar. When future generations passed that place, the Israelites were to recall the great works of God (Joshua 4).

In both Scripture and life, failures in faith are often failures of memory. When hard times come and the memory of God's greatness and God's work in our lives fades, we are tempted to turn to other things—idols—to fill the gap. We can resist such spiritual amnesia through continued practices of Scripture study and prayer.

In corporate worship, together we sing and study the great acts of God. In addition, Jesus gave us a most profound aid for remembering—the Lord's Supper. "Do this in remembrance of Me" (Luke 22:19).

we reject God as Creator—or attempt to *use* God for our purposes—and we *worship* aspects of creation or the products of our hands.[1]

The prophet Isaiah presents a sustained and devastating attack on humankind's idolatrous instincts in chapters 44—46. Beginning in chapter 40, Isaiah spoke of one of the lowest points in Israel's history: the Babylonian exile (597–538 B.C.). In this event, the unthinkable happened. The Southern kingdom of Judah had fallen. Jerusalem was destroyed. The temple was leveled. The ark of God was lost from history. Nebuchadnezzar dragged the best and brightest of Judah as captives and exiles to Babylon. We could easily forgive the outside observer who might have assumed this was the last anyone would hear of Israel and their defeated God, *Yahweh*.

Into this situation, Isaiah made some remarkable claims. Rather than viewing the Exile as the defeat of *Yahweh*, Isaiah reminded the people of the greatness of the one God of creation. God had not been defeated, and neither had God's plan been thwarted. Instead, Isaiah presented one of the most profound and sustained descriptions of the greatness of God. God stands over the idols, over the wise, over creation, over political powers, and over history.

Given God's greatness, Isaiah reminded Israel to resist the allure of idolatry surrounding them in Babylon. The temptation would certainly have been strong. It appeared the Babylonians had won the decisive victory and that God's protection and care had failed. The old rules and ways contained in the Torah would not have seemed to apply to their current situation. They were living in a powerful culture that embraced idols. The temptation to join in this worship would have been highly appealing. Idol worship provides the great benefit of a god that is tangible. A statue-god is always there, right where you place it. With idol worship, the (false) hope was that if you make the right sacrifices—in some cultures that even meant child sacrifices—the god would respond with what the worshiper wanted. Idolatry thus provides an illusion of control over the divine—a control that is foreign to the worship of Yahweh. In these changed circumstances Israel faced in the Exile, *Yahweh* surely seemed far away, indeed.

In this context, Isaiah leveled his attack on idolatrous practices. In chapter 44 he highlighted the folly and deep irony of creating idols. In 44:9–17 he described the process of chopping down a tree, making a fire with part of the wood, fashioning a god with another piece, and falling down in worship with the cry, "Deliver me, for you are my god" (Isaiah 44:17).

In chapter 46, Isaiah mocked the Babylonian idols, which not only failed to save, but also required a cart and pack animals to move them. Isaiah 46:2 pictures these idols in the back of a cart, showing the captivity of these powerless gods. In 46:5, God asked the rhetorical question about comparing him to such powerless things.

In an echo of chapter 44, Isaiah 46 again looks at the process of forming idols in another way. Instead of wood, precious gold and silver are taken to the silversmith, who forms them into a shape. The people fall down in worship of the result (Isa. 46:6). I can imagine them struggling to lift the burden onto their shoulders to stagger home with their immobile god. Presumably they consult with their wives about where it would look best in the house, as it certainly was not going to move on its own (Isa. 46:7). Then the family has a crisis and cries out to their statue. The language reflects Elijah's showdown with the prophets of Baal in 1 Kings 18. Elijah stood to the side, mocking their feverish efforts to coax a response with their cries to their so-called god. In the climax of 46:7, Isaiah highlighted the failure of such an idol to deliver—*Yahweh's* key role in the Old Testament.

These gods are immobile, dependent, silent, and powerless. They stand in stark contrast to *Yahweh* and his works in speaking creation into being, forming a people, and performing great acts of deliverance. The antidote for such idolatrous tendencies comes in Isaiah 46:8–9: "Remember this," "recall it to mind," and "remember the former things." The worship of Yahweh is relevant in any situation. No matter how distant God may seem, we are to retain the memories of God's great acts of deliverance and move forward in confidence of God's work to come.

Idolatry in the New Testament (Acts 17:24–31)

Idolatry continued in the New Testament, and Paul confronted it directly in the encounter with the philosophers in Athens while on his second missionary journey. Paul observed that Athens was filled with idols. Acts 17:16 reports Paul's reaction: "his spirit was being provoked within him." Verse 17 describes Paul's ministry in Athens as "reasoning in the synagogue with the Jews and the God-fearing Gentiles, and in the market place every day with those who happened to be present." The former—the synagogue—was the setting for his typical ministry practice, but the latter depicts Paul as a first-century Socrates, walking through the marketplace, reasoning with people.

In the course of this activity, Paul encountered representatives of two of the prominent philosophical schools of the ancient world: Epicureans and Stoics. These two groups were very different from each other. Epicureans rejected the old Roman gods. If there was a god, they believed he was too far removed from people to make any kind of difference. The pursuit of pleasure was the main goal of life for them. The Stoics, on the other hand, believed God was everywhere—and reason dominated their view of the universe.[2]

Paul was not too impressed by Athens in this meeting, and these groups were underwhelmed by Paul. Some dismissed Paul as a "babbler"—an intellectual loafer who knew just enough to get himself in trouble. Others actually took the time to listen to the content of Paul's message.

Verses 22–31 report Paul's message. What Paul did serves as a crucial model for anyone seeking to convey the gospel. Paul did not simply proclaim religious jargon, and neither did he berate the Athenians for their religious ignorance. Rather, he took something they understood and used it as a bridge from their culture to the gospel. Paul referred to their shrine, inscribed "TO AN UNKNOWN GOD" (17:23) and used it as a platform to describe *Yahweh*.

In verse 24, Paul repeated the Genesis 1:1 declaration of God's unlimited domain. I imagine Paul sweeping his hands toward the Acropolis and other great edifices of Athens with the comment that God "does not

Recognizing the Bigness of God

- Take an honest inventory of your life to identify those things that may be idols for you.
- Make some practical and tangible changes in your time management and your budget to make sure God is over all.
- Commit to regular practices of Scripture study and prayer to enhance your spiritual memory of God's greatness.

dwell in temples made with hands" (Acts 17:24). Further, rather than needing or being in some way dependent on our sacrifices, God is the One who provides all things for life (17:25). What God does desire is that we seek him, find him (17:27), and repent (17:30)—thus preparing us for the judgment to come. Verse 29 provides the corrective to idolatrous practices, returning to the picture from Isaiah of the shaping of gold, silver, or stone in creating idols that pale in comparison to the true, living God.

Implications and Actions: Idolatry Today

While citizens of twenty-first century American culture are unlikely to form statues and believe they bear the power of God, we still have our idols. We are just as likely as the exiled Israelites and the Athenian philosophers to offer what belongs to God to someone or something else. As God's people we must preserve the *bigness* of God in our worship, lives, understanding, and imagination by guarding against idolatry.

Several years ago when leading a study of Isaiah 44—46 in our church, I distributed sheets of paper and asked those present to write down an idol with which our culture struggles. The top three responses were money, materialism/possessions, and television. Other responses were sports, family, pleasure/self-satisfaction, home, job, power, popularity, recreation, and sex.

What are other idols for us? One Bible scholar has suggested that the prime sources of idols lie in things that entice us, things we fear, things we need, and things we trust.[3] Our idols may be our occupations and skills, science and technology, political affiliations, patriotism, or trust in our financial status. These may be good things—or even great things. When we take them out of their proper place, however, they take what belongs to God and reduce God's greatness in our lives and worship.

The Isaiah and Acts passages also provide good examples for us in engaging with idolatry and properly dealing with it. Isaiah was speaking to Israel, God's people, who should have known better. He directly and even provocatively critiqued the folly of it all. He was seeking to awaken Israel from their slide into idolatrous error. We should be ruthless with ourselves in rooting out our idolatries as believers. In engaging with the Athenians, however, Paul took a very different approach. He started with their culture and reasoned with them, pointing to the greatness of God and the resulting implications for life. As people with a mission to share the gospel with others, we should be students of their culture and should be seeking to build bridges of understanding to the gospel.

How great is the Lord? God alone is worthy of our exclusive worship and devotion. That proper ordering of life is crucial for all areas of our lives. Your mother may have told you, "You are what you eat." In a sense, *we are what we worship.* We can never *be* God, but we can become more holy through proper worship of the living God, expressed in our praise, our work, our relationships, our finances, and our time. On the other hand, we can worship what is beneath us and degrade ourselves. Our involvement with God's mission must rest on the firm foundation of our great God.

QUESTIONS

1. What are some idols in our culture?

2. What are some idols for American Christianity?

3. In light of God's unlimited domain, what areas of life are you holding back from God's rule and lordship?

4. What are some bridges to the gospel for our unchurched neighbors or coworkers?

NOTES

1. Christopher J. H. Wright, *The Mission of God: Unlocking the Bible's Grand Narrative* (Downers Grove, Illinois: IVP Academic, 2006), 165.
2. I. Howard Marshall, *Acts,* Tyndale New Testament Commentaries (Grand Rapids, Michigan: Eerdmans Press, 1980), 284.
3. Wright, 165–169.

LESSON TWO
The Mission's Motivation

FOCAL TEXTS
Deuteronomy 7:7–8;
Psalm 136:1–11, 23–26;
Jonah 3:10—4:3, 9–11;
John 3:16; Romans 5:6–8

BACKGROUND
Deuteronomy 7:7–8; Psalm 136;
Jonah; John 3:16; Romans 5:6–8

MAIN IDEA
God's love is the motivation for reaching out to the world.

QUESTIONS TO EXPLORE
What motivates God to care about the world? What motivates you?

STUDY AIM
To evaluate my approach to the people of the world in light of the Bible's teachings about God's love

QUICK READ
Throughout the Bible we find God's love for the world motivating God's work. Our role in God's mission is to carry that love to others.

Throughout the centuries Christians have struggled with profound, mind-bending questions when it comes to God and the universe. How do we comprehend eternity? How long was God's beginning before creation? How do we reconcile a sovereign God with free will? Why did God create in the first place? While these questions can spark endless discussion and debate, God truly is so vast and infinite that our limited minds will never be able to wrap around him—beyond what God has chosen to reveal to us in Scripture and creation. While we can only make guesses about many such questions, we have hints about the last one based on God's dealings with us. Motivating God's relationship with us is a powerful, committed, and transforming love. In his first letter, John makes that simple, yet profound statement: "God is love" (1 John 4:8).

Love, however, is surely one of the most overused words in the English language. During any given day we may assert that we *love* family, chocolate, a favorite athletic team, an outfit, friends, or a certain television show. We treat this one English word like an overburdened pack animal on which we pile more and more baggage. Complicating matters, many in our culture talk vaguely of God and love, and yet they reject the biblical depiction of God as loving. They seem to believe that a loving God should not have an opinion about how we happen to live our lives. Others see love as the theme of the New Testament but view the Old Testament as simply law and judgment. One of the earliest Christian heretics, Marcion, attracted quite a movement by rejecting the Old Testament as the work of a different God, entirely. A careful look at the whole sweep of Scripture, however, clearly shows that a deep and profound love lies at the heart of God's relationship with us and God's mission for the world.

DEUTERONOMY 7:7–8

7"The Lord did not set His love on you nor choose you because you were more in number than any of the peoples, for you were the fewest of all peoples, 8but because the Lord loved you and kept the oath which He swore to your forefathers, the Lord brought you out by a mighty hand and redeemed you from the house of slavery, from the hand of Pharaoh king of Egypt.

Psalm 136:1–11, 23–26

¹Give thanks to the Lord, for He is good,
  For His lovingkindness is everlasting.
²Give thanks to the God of gods,
  For His lovingkindness is everlasting.
³Give thanks to the Lord of lords,
  For His lovingkindness is everlasting.
⁴To Him who alone does great wonders,
  For His lovingkindness is everlasting;
⁵To Him who made the heavens with skill,
  For His lovingkindness is everlasting;
⁶To Him who spread out the earth above the waters,
  For His lovingkindness is everlasting;
⁷To Him who made the great lights,
  For His lovingkindness is everlasting:
⁸The sun to rule by day,
  For His lovingkindness is everlasting,
⁹The moon and stars to rule by night,
  For His lovingkindness is everlasting.
¹⁰To Him who smote the Egyptians in their firstborn,
  For His lovingkindness is everlasting,
¹¹And brought Israel out from their midst,
For His lovingkindness is everlasting,

. . . .

²³Who remembered us in our low estate,
  For His lovingkindness is everlasting,
  ²⁴And has rescued us from our adversaries,
  For His lovingkindness is everlasting;
  ²⁵Who gives food to all flesh,
  For His lovingkindness is everlasting.
  ²⁶Give thanks to the God of heaven,
  For His lovingkindness is everlasting.

JONAH 3:10—4:3, 9–11

¹⁰ When God saw their deeds, that they turned from their wicked way, then God relented concerning the calamity which He had declared He would bring upon them. And He did not do it.

⁴:¹ But it greatly displeased Jonah and he became angry. ² He prayed to the Lord and said, "Please Lord, was not this what I said while I was still in my own country? Therefore in order to forestall this I fled to Tarshish, for I knew that You are a gracious and compassionate God, slow to anger and abundant in lovingkindness, and one who relents concerning calamity. ³ "Therefore now, O Lord, please take my life from me, for death is better to me than life."

. . . .

⁹ Then God said to Jonah, "Do you have good reason to be angry about the plant?" And he said, "I have good reason to be angry, even to death." ¹⁰ Then the Lord said, "You had compassion on the plant for which you did not work and which you did not cause to grow, which came up overnight and perished overnight. ¹¹ "Should I not have compassion on Nineveh, the great city in which there are more than 120,000 persons who do not know the difference between their right and left hand, as well as many animals?"

JOHN 3:16

"For God so loved the world, that He gave His only begotten Son, that whoever believes in Him shall not perish, but have eternal life.

ROMANS 5:6–8

⁶ For while we were still helpless, at the right time Christ died for the ungodly. ⁷ For one will hardly die for a righteous man; though perhaps for the good man someone would dare even to die. ⁸ But God demonstrates His own love toward us, in that while we were yet sinners, Christ died for us.

God's Lovingkindness

Both Psalm 136 and Jonah refer to God's *lovingkindness*. Other common translations include *love, steadfast love, mercy,* or *faithful love*. Beneath our English translations lies what many believe is the most important Hebrew word in the Old Testament: *hesed*. No single word in English captures the richness and depth of *hesed*. It is used many times in the Old Testament for both human relationships and relationships with God.

In Joshua 2, Rahab helped the Israelite spies in Jericho and pleaded, "Since I have dealt kindly [*hesed*], that you also will deal kindly [*hesed*] with my father's household" (Joshua 2:12). Jonah 3:10—4:3, 9–11 refers to *hesed* as a part of God's nature in dealing with us. God revealed this nature powerfully in Exodus 34 and the revelation to Moses of God's nature. "The Lord, the Lord God, compassionate and gracious, slow to anger, and abounding in lovingkindness [*hesed*] and truth" (Exodus 34:6–7).

Hesed is covenant love, committed love, faithfulness, loyalty, and a determined love that transcends our acts of rejection.[1] Let us rejoice in God's *hesed* to us, and may we reflect *hesed* in our relationships with others!

God's Love and Salvation (John 3:16)

The most famous verse in Scripture, John 3:16, proclaims with great clarity the motivation of God's work through Christ. We are so familiar with this verse that we sometimes lose sight of its context in the flow of the conversation with the Pharisee, Nicodemus.

John described Nicodemus in 3:1 as "a ruler of the Jews." This likely reflects his membership on the ruling council—the Sanhedrin. From Nicodemus's esteemed perspective, salvation came through birth as a Jew and through strict observance of the law and rabbinic traditions.

Jesus shocked Nicodemus in verse 5 with the statement that salvation comes through a new birth. What birth could be better than his birth as a Jew? Verse 9 reveals the depth of his confusion: "How can these things be?"

Jesus explained in John 3:16 that this salvation flows from the love of God for the world. Nicodemus may have been shocked again at this statement that God loved "the world." God's love for Israel—and more specifically for the righteous in Israel—would not have been in doubt for him. The statement of God's love for the *world*, however, may have surprised him. In reality, though, "For God so loved the world" could be the opening phrase of the Bible or the prefix for any of God's great works in the Old and New Testament. That love drives the action of God in reaching out to us.

The Outline of God's Love (Psalm 136:1–11, 23–26)

Psalm 136 is an unmistakable expression of worship and a reminder that the Psalter is the hymnbook of Israel. With its repeated refrain, "For His lovingkindness is everlasting," I imagine a form of responsive reading in worship.

The first nine verses focus on the nature and greatness of God and the wonders of creation (recall lesson one). Verses 10–11 point back to the greatest event in the Old Testament, the deliverance of God in the Exodus. The last few verses of the psalm turn from God, creation, and national deliverance to "us." Part of God's enduring love lies in his *remembering* us (Psalm 136:23), *rescuing* us (Ps. 136:24), and *providing* for us (136:25). These signs or markers of God's love in Psalm 136 show a wide sweep of God's work. God's love lies not in warm feelings for us. The results of God's love are creation, deliverance, remembering, and providing.

IF GOD REALLY LOVES US

If God really loves us, then
- why is there judgment and hell?
- why would I need to change my lifestyle or practices?
- why do bad things happen to us?

We encounter such questions in daytime talk shows, popular culture, and conversations with family, friends, or co-workers. How can today's focal passages help address these questions and the true nature of God and love?

God's Love for All (Deuteronomy 7:7–8; Jonah 3:10—4:3, 9–11)

If Nicodemus was surprised by Jesus' statement of God's love for the world, it was because Nicodemus's community had overlooked or deemphasized some clear statements in the Old Testament. God's love for the world can be seen clearly in the Old Testament. One struggle for Israel, though, was remembering that God's love reached beyond their nation or people to all nations and all people.

Deuteronomy 7:7–8. The most well-known verse of the Old Testament in Jewish life was the *Shema*, Deuteronomy 6:4. It is the John 3:16 of the Old Testament. "Hear, O Israel! The Lord is our God, the Lord is one!" This verse and the ones following provide bedrock teaching about God, the great commandment to love God, and remembering this teaching through life and through the generations.

Deuteronomy 7 turns to basic teaching for life in the Promised Land, with warnings against following Canaanite religions. Verse 6 makes a clear statement about the role of Israel as God's people: "For you are a holy people to the Lord your God; the Lord your God has chosen you to be a people for His own possession out of all the peoples who are on the face of the earth." Hearing such a statement from the one, true God could be a source of pride. Before their heads swelled or their buttons burst, however, verses 7–8 provided the reminder. God did not choose them because of their extra goodness, their high moral character relative to others, or their native strength. God's love for them comes from God's broader purposes. God's love for his people is in service to his love for the world. That fact shines clearly in the story of that most famous of the minor prophets: Jonah.

Jonah 3:10—4:3, 9–11. Jonah was a prophet in the eighth century B.C. in the Northern kingdom. In the Old Testament we find one other reference to Jonah, in 2 Kings 14:25, where Jonah had prophesied about the success of King Jeroboam in restoring the borders of Israel. That was the kind of prophesying I believe Jonah liked. It spoke to the success of his people—God's people—Israel. What we find in Jonah 1 is a very different assignment. In 1:2 God said this: "Arise, go to Nineveh the great city and cry against it, for their wickedness has come up before Me."

Nineveh was the capital of Assyria, the most dreaded and brutal empire of that day. They were refined only in their creative techniques of torture. About 100 years later, the Assyrians would entirely wipe out the Northern kingdom of Israel. Jonah would not have been surprised in the least that their wickedness had offended the Lord. Jonah was evidently surprised that God would care for their repentance and would waste Jonah's prophetic time on them.

By the end of chapter 3, Jonah had fled and been fetched back on task by the big fish. Jonah proclaimed God's message in Nineveh with spectacular success. Jonah's true feelings and God's true love for the world shine through in 4:2. Jonah accurately described God's character in 4:2, echoing the great self-revelation of God to Moses on Mount Sinai in Exodus 34:6–7. The problem with God's love and grace from Jonah's perspective (and perhaps from ours) is that Jonah wanted God's love, grace, and lovingkindness for himself and his people only. For others, he wanted justice and judgment. The surprising truth of the Book of Jonah is God's love for Gentiles—and the worst of Gentiles at that. God, indeed, loves the world. That love was the basis for God's mission for Nineveh and Jonah's role in that mission.

The Nature of God's Love (Romans 5:6–8)

After Christ, some still clung to the idea of God's exclusive love for Israel. The Spirit's movement in the Book of Acts, however, shattered the ancient barriers between Jews, Samaritans, and Gentiles. ". . . God so loved the world" that God's mission reaches out to all. In Romans 5 Paul spoke to two crucial aspects of that love.

In the first four chapters of Romans, Paul laid out his theology. He started with the righteousness of God, revealed in the gospel. He then turned to the brokenness of humanity. Both Gentile (Romans 1) and Jew (Rom. 2) are included, leading up to that famous verse, "For all have sinned and fall short of the glory of God" (3:23). The solution to this problem lies in the work of Christ. We can be justified—made right with God—by faith. In chapter 4 Paul used the example of Abraham. "Abraham believed God, and it was credited to him as righteousness" (4:3). The end of chapter 4 makes the same connection for us. By faith in Jesus, such righteousness is credited to us.

Chapter 5 starts with a key transition word, "Therefore." The first 11 verses of Romans 5 contain wonders of theological depth. A key theme, however, is the incredible love of God. In verse 8, Paul proclaimed that

God's love is *demonstrated* love. It is not that God has nice feelings of affection for us. Rather, God's love is demonstrated on a cross in a massive act of sacrifice for us.

God's love in Romans 5 is also *transforming* love. Before Christ we were "helpless" (5:6), "ungodly" (5:6), "sinners" (5:8), and "enemies" (5:10). God did not wait until we were holy, righteous, and lovable to save us. Instead, when we were still helpless, powerless, sinners, and enemies, God acted on our behalf. The transforming power of God's love shines through. Now, according to Romans 5, we have "peace with God" (5:1), "introduction by faith into this grace" (5:2), and the opportunity to "exult" in grace (5:2) and in suffering (5:3). In addition we now have hope (5:4–5) and salvation (5:9–10). God's love transforms us and results in wholeness and salvation.

For Life Today: God's Love, God's Mission, and Our Mission

We know that God is all-powerful, all-knowing, and eternal. I believe it is legitimate, however, to see a certain vulnerability of God in creating us, loving us, and giving us freedom. We can read the story of Scripture as a love story—of Creator for humanity. This love has transcended rejection after rejection on our part. This is a demonstrated love that pursued us all the way to the cross.

As recipients of this love and salvation, we are to show this love to others. Many times we speak about missions in terms of obligation, obedience, mandate, or demands. Perhaps we need to return to the motivation behind God's mission: love. With God and with us, mission is the result of love. To truly love others is to want God's best for them. Helping others to understand and experience God's best is another way to describe *missions*.

QUESTIONS

1. How does our culture understand love? How is that different from biblical love?

2. Who is Nineveh to you? Who are the people you believe to be beyond the reach of the gospel or of God's love?

3. How can we demonstrate our love for others?

4. How can our mission be a lifestyle of love rather than a chore?

5. If you wrote your personal Psalm 136, what statements would you write to lead to that refrain, "For His lovingkindness is everlasting?"

NOTES

1. D. K Stuart, "Steadfast Love," in *The International Standard Bible Encyclopedia: Volume Four, Q-Z*, ed. Geoffrey W. Bromiley (Grand Rapids, Michigan: Eerdmans Publishing Company, 1988), 613–614.

LESSON THREE
The Mission's Focus

FOCAL TEXTS
Genesis 12:1–3;
Exodus 19:1–6; Luke 1:46–55

BACKGROUND
Genesis 12:1–7; Exodus 19:1–6;
Matthew 1:1; Luke 1:25–56

MAIN IDEA
God chose to work through one man and one people to bring the fullness of God's blessing to all people in Jesus.

QUESTION TO EXPLORE
What does God's call to Abraham have to do with me?

STUDY AIM
To understand the significance for God's mission and my life of God's call to Abraham

QUICK READ
God's method in carrying out God's mission is calling some to bear the message to all. Abraham serves as the pattern followed by Israel, Jesus, and us.

Imagine you are stuck waiting for a flight in a crowded airport terminal (not too much of a stretch, these days), and the person sitting beside you strikes up a conversation. What do you talk about?

"So, are you going home or leaving home?"

"Oh, you're from Fort Worth? My second cousin lives in Arlington. Maybe you know him?"

You may have had this type of conversation. After a pause, the next question is usually, "Well, what do you do?" We all tend to define ourselves or one another by occupations.

After sharing about your work, you reciprocate, "What about you?"

Imagine the new acquaintance responding, "I'm a pilot."

"Oh, that's interesting," you say, "What do you fly?"

"Nothing," is the response.

That strikes you as strange, and so you probe a little deeper. "Well, do you fly for one of the airlines?"

"Nope."

Still trying to work this out, you ask, "Are you retired?"

"Oh, no! That's not for me. Not yet, anyway."

It would not take very long for the conversation to grind to a halt as you try to understand how someone could be a pilot without flying anywhere or flying anything! Either you or he has an incorrect understanding of what a pilot is.

Could it be that the same kind of situation exists for someone who claims to be a Christian but is not on God's mission? Being a Christian and being on God's mission go together. Christians are to live the task of sharing the gospel with their words and with their actions. A Christian not on God's mission is a contradiction in terms. The reason these go together is tied deeply to the way God has chosen to work, revealed in Scripture.

GENESIS 12:1–3

¹Now the Lord said to Abram, "Go forth from your country,
And from your relatives
And from your father's house,

To the land which I will show you;
²And I will make you a great nation,
And I will bless you,
And make your name great;
And so you shall be a blessing;
³And I will bless those who bless you,
And the one who curses you I will curse.
And in you all the families of the earth will be blessed."

EXODUS 19:1–6

¹In the third month after the sons of Israel had gone out of the land of Egypt, on that very day they came into the wilderness of Sinai. ²When they set out from Rephidim, they came to the wilderness of Sinai and camped in the wilderness; and there Israel camped in front of the mountain. ³Moses went up to God, and the Lord called to him from the mountain, saying, "Thus you shall say to the house of Jacob and tell the sons of Israel: ⁴`You yourselves have seen what I did to the Egyptians, and how I bore you on eagles' wings, and brought you to Myself. ⁵`Now then, if you will indeed obey My voice and keep My covenant, then you shall be My own possession among all the peoples, for all the earth is Mine; ⁶and you shall be to Me a kingdom of priests and a holy nation.' These are the words that you shall speak to the sons of Israel."

LUKE 1:46–55

⁴⁶And Mary said:
"My soul exalts the Lord,
⁴⁷And my spirit has rejoiced in God my Savior.
⁴⁸"For He has had regard for the humble state of His bondslave;
For behold, from this time on all generations will count me blessed.
⁴⁹"For the Mighty One has done great things for me;
And holy is His name.

> ⁵⁰"And His mercy is upon generation after generation
> Toward those who fear Him.
> ⁵¹"He has done mighty deeds with His arm;
> He has scattered those who were proud in the thoughts of their heart.
> ⁵²"He has brought down rulers from their thrones,
> And has exalted those who were humble.
> ⁵³"He has filled the hungry with good things;
> And sent away the rich empty-handed.
> ⁵⁴"He has given help to Israel His servant,
> In remembrance of His mercy,
> ⁵⁵As He spoke to our fathers,
> To Abraham and his descendants forever."

The Model of God's Work: Abraham (Genesis 12:1–3)

Genesis 12 marks a turning point in Scripture. Everything that follows is different because of these verses. In the first few chapters of Genesis, God speaks creation into being, and then humanity quickly rejects God. Adam and Eve sin, and Cain kills Abel. The rampant sinfulness of humanity leads to the Flood. While Noah and his family seem to have a new start, the sinful nature of humankind has not changed.[1] In chapter 11, the tower of Babel represents idolatrous and rebellious intentions. Creation appears to have spun out of control.

At this point we could imagine several options for God. God could have finished destroying his disappointing creation. He could have forced our wills and removed our ability to rebel. Instead, God did something exceedingly strange in these opening verses of Genesis 12. God called a seventy-five-year-old childless man to leave his homeland and his extended family and to go to a strange land to become a great nation. This seemingly insignificant event set in motion the rest of the storyline of Scripture. Abraham's calling also helps us understand a concept in Scripture that is both important and misunderstood: the idea of election.

> ## COVENANT
>
> Genesis 12, Exodus 19, and the ministry of Jesus all intersect the crucial biblical idea of *covenant*. The original Hebrew word for *covenant* literally means either "eat bread with" or "to bind or fetter."[2] Both ideas fit with the ideas of relationship and bond. Covenants were a common part of relationship in the ancient world, and the Bible takes this idea and uses it as a metaphor for our relationship with God. Covenants with God in Scripture include the covenant of the rainbow with Noah (Genesis 9), the covenant of circumcision with Abraham (Genesis 17), and the covenant with Israel (Exodus 19).
>
> Much of the Old Testament describes the Hebrews' struggle to keep the covenant and the negative consequences of failure. The prophet Jeremiah glimpsed a crucial vision of God's work in Christ when he described a "new covenant" (Jeremiah 31:33). Jesus then set his ministry of grace in this context at the Lord's Supper: "This cup which is poured out for you is the new covenant in My blood" (Luke 22:20).

Many struggle with the concept of election because it seems unfair that God would choose some over others. When parents favor one child over another, we label the family as dysfunctional. That is what Scripture seems to some to imply about God—that God favors some of his people over others. "Jacob I loved, but Esau I hated" (Romans 9:13). When this idea is pressed to the extreme, we end up with the idea that God makes some people for heaven and others for hell.

It is at this point, however, where some have misread the idea of election. The mistake is viewing God's choice solely as election to benefit or salvation: *If I am the elect, then I am saved, and I will go to heaven. The others won't.* Scripture does not describe God's call in this way. In these opening verses of Genesis 12, God promised some great things to Abraham: a nation from him; blessings on him; a great name; and protection against the "curse" of others. If this were all God had said, then election is the lottery, and Abraham just won it.

God continued, however, "And so you shall be a blessing. . . . And in you all the families of the earth will be blessed" (12:2–3). These sentences give us God's purpose. They also give us a clue about how God works in the world. God desires to bless everyone, and God does it through relationships. God's call to Abraham represents an election for God's mission. God conscripted Abraham for God's purposes. God did not choose Abraham because God loved him more than anyone else. God chose Abraham because God loves everyone else. From the point of that calling and Abraham's obedience, Abraham's life was lived in service of that love. He obviously benefited from this with a powerful relationship with God. At the same time, however, Abraham's life from that point on was anything but easy. He spent the rest of his days wandering, unsettled, and on the move. He lived under God's purpose and plan. This pattern of action in choosing for mission recurs throughout Scripture from the patriarchs to Israel to Christ and to us.

Being called by God is not the ticket to an easy or successful life. Answering the call is the way to a purposeful life lived serving God and God's mission.

Israel's Role in God's Mission (Exodus 19:1–6)

In Genesis 1, God spoke creation into being. In calling Abraham, God spoke the people of ancient Israel into being. Israel's history through the Old Testament carries on the promise of Abraham and bears the same purpose. The Israelites were not chosen by God because of their inherent lovability or godly character. Neither were they chosen for their personal prosperity. Israel was chosen for God's purpose and mission.

Exodus 19 describes Israel's special role. This passage comes at a crucial point in Exodus and in Israel's history. In Exodus 12 God sent

> ### EMBRACING THE MISSION
>
> - List your personal spheres of influence. These may include such entities as your workplace, your relationships with friends and family, and your neighborhood.
> - Honestly compare your actions and influence in those circles to that of a non-Christian. Is your faith making a difference?
> - Take tangible steps to show Christ's love in those places.

the final, devastating plague on Egypt and Pharaoh, and the Hebrew people were set free. In chapter 14 they crossed the sea, and the pursuing Egyptians were swept away. In the ensuing chapters, God provided water, manna, and deliverance in battle against the Amalekites. In 19:1 the people came to Mount Sinai.

We might read Exodus 19 as the vows of a marriage ceremony. God was sketching the outline for his relationship with his people. In these crucial opening verses of Exodus 19, God recounted all he had done for them in the past, and he bound himself to them for the future with his covenant. The Hebrews were to obey—"keep My covenant" (Exodus 19:5). God's part would be to make them "My own possession," "a kingdom of priests and a holy nation" (Exod.19:6).

God promised Israel these wonderful blessings. They would be his treasured possession. The blessings of this covenant were not given, however, for them to sit back and enjoy. On the contrary, they were given a task as well. They were to be a "kingdom of priests"—a responsibility Israel often overlooked. Priests exist to bring others to God. Israel was chosen to bear God's love to all people and to mediate that love for others. Too often, Israel fell into the trap of thinking they were chosen because they were special or for their own benefit. They were chosen for God's purposes and for God's mission that all might know God.

Jeremiah even made the comment that Israel's failure in their part of the covenant inhibited God's mission to the world: "'If you will return, O Israel,' declared the LORD, 'Then you should return to Me. And if you will put away your detested things from My presence, And will not waver, And you will swear, 'As the LORD lives,' in truth, in justice and in righteousness; *Then the nations will bless themselves in Him, and in Him they will glory*'" (Jeremiah 4:1–2, italics added for emphasis). Following in the stream from Abraham, Israel was elect, not for their personal benefit, but for God's mission in the world.

Jesus and God's Mission (Luke 1:46–55)

Jesus' life and mission stands as the fulfillment and continuation of the promise to Abraham, and Jesus also continues the pattern of election to mission. In fact, the opening verse of Matthew clearly connects Jesus with Abraham: "The record of the genealogy of Jesus the Messiah, the son of David, the son of Abraham" (Matthew 1:1). Mary's great song of praise, known as the Magnificat, in Luke 1:46–55 does the same.

The Magnificat comes in the wonderful flow of events leading to the birth of Christ. Zacharias received an angelic visitation about the promise of a son, John the Baptist. Then so did Mary, about the promise of Jesus' birth. In Luke 1:39, Mary visited Elizabeth, the wife of Zacharias. Elizabeth's unborn son (John) "leaped" at the presence of Mary (Luke 1:41). The Holy Spirit inspired an exclamation of praise from Elizabeth (Luke 1:41–45), and Mary responded with the Magnificat (Luke 1:46–55).

Mary's words reflect the song of Hannah in 1 Samuel 2:1–10. Both Mary and Hannah spoke strong words about God's plan, which turns things upside-down (Luke 1:51–53). Her last phrase, in 1:55, connects God's work with Christ to God's prior work with Abraham and the great promise to Abraham. Jesus fulfilled the promise of Genesis 12 that through Abraham all people would be blessed. Jesus would also fulfill the role of Israel—the perfect, sinless Israel.

Abraham and Us: Called for Mission

Our involvement with God's mission did not start with the Great Commission (Matthew 28:18–20). We are a part of God's unfolding plan, the outlines of which we find in Genesis 12:1–3. Like Abraham, Israel, and Jesus, our calling is not for our own benefit. As God's people, we are to serve God's mission. Once we make the confession, "Jesus is Lord," we find salvation, healing, peace, and *mission*. They go together. It is not the case that some are ordinary Christians and others are the special models made for missions. *Every* Christian is to be a part of God's plan that God would be known. While not all of us are called to foreign missions, all are called to bear the message of the Gospel and to show God's love to others.

God could have chosen to spread his message and to restore broken humanity in any number of ways. God's plan from the beginning, however, has been to spread his story from one life to the next. One life comes under God's calling to spread the word to the next. Leave it to God to create a plan that depends so crucially on us! In doing so, God

LESSON 3: *The Mission's Focus* 43

has created the perfect balance between his will and human freedom and between his sovereignty and our actions. As a result, as Christians we are the elect. Like Abraham, we are elect for the purposes of God and God's mission. Along with Abraham, we are called to *go*, so that the whole world can experience the wonder and glory of God's grace. Anyone who claims to be a pilot flies something, and anyone who claims to follow Christ is on Christ's mission.

QUESTIONS

1. What are the barriers that keep us from obeying God like Abraham did?

2. How do we try to accept the benefits of being God's people while avoiding the calling and mission?

3. How has God equipped and placed you to share his word with others?

4. Are you willing to go wherever God calls you?

NOTES

1. The descriptions of humanity from before the Flood in Genesis 6:5 ("every intent of the thoughts of his heart was only evil continually") and after the Flood in Genesis 8:21 ("the intent of man's heart is evil from his youth") are similar.
2. D.F. Estes, "Covenant," *The International Standard Bible Encyclopedia: Volume One, A-D*, ed. Geoffrey W. Bromiley (Grand Rapids, Michigan: Eerdmans Publishing Company, 1988), 790.

LESSON FOUR
The Mission's Unlimited Reach

FOCAL TEXTS
Genesis 12:1–3;
Isaiah 49:5–6; Luke 2:25–32;
Acts 1:8; Romans 10:12–13

BACKGROUND
Genesis 12:1–3;
Isaiah 49:1–6;
Luke 2:21–35; Acts 1:1–8;
Romans 10:5–13

MAIN IDEA
God's mission extends to all people.

QUESTION TO EXPLORE
Who are the people in our world for whom God does not care?

STUDY AIM
To identify ways in which I will participate in God's mission to all people wherever and however God leads me

QUICK READ
From beginning to end in Scripture, God's plan has been for all people to know him. We play a crucial role in that plan.

Pronouns are important: *I, me, we, us, you, she, he, they, them*. They can reveal a lot about a speaker or writer. For example, you may know people who are the hero of all their stories and have a favorite subject: themselves. Their speech is richly populated with *me, mine,* and *I*. Our choice of pronouns can also reveal our attitudes. From time to time our dogs will indulge in the kitchen trash, depositing coffee grounds and chewed-up food wrappers throughout the house. In exasperation I may say to my wife, "Look at what *your* dogs have done." She then uses pronouns to remind *me* of *my* connection with *our* canines.

Two very important sets of pronouns speak to the heart of who we are and how we view others: *we/us* and *they/them*. When we talk about *we/us* at the most basic level, which *we* do we mean? Is the most important *we* our family, our nation, our race, or our identity as believers in Jesus Christ? When we talk about *they/them* do we speak with respect, or are there certain groups of whom we speak with scorn and contempt?

Scripture has important implications for such pronouns—both in how we understand our own identity and in how we are to deal with others. According to Scripture, the most important component of our identity—our most important *we*—should be our identity as followers of Christ. Additionally, our stance toward those who are not believers should be one of seeking to show the love, compassion, and truth of the gospel, for God clearly wants *all* people to know him.

Genesis 12:1–3

^{12:1}Now the Lord said to Abram, "Go forth from your country, And from your relatives And from your father's house, To the land which I will show you; ²And I will make you a great nation, And I will bless you, And make your name great; And so you shall be a blessing; ³And I will bless those who bless you, And the one who curses you I will curse. And in you all the families of the earth will be blessed."

Isaiah 49:5–6

⁵And now says the Lord, who formed Me from the womb to be His Servant, To bring Jacob back to Him, so that Israel might

be gathered to Him (For I am honored in the sight of the Lord, And My God is My strength), ⁶He says, "It is too small a thing that You should be My Servant To raise up the tribes of Jacob and to restore the preserved ones of Israel; I will also make You a light of the nations So that My salvation may reach to the end of the earth."

LUKE 2:25–32

²⁵And there was a man in Jerusalem whose name was Simeon; and this man was righteous and devout, looking for the consolation of Israel; and the Holy Spirit was upon him. ²⁶And it had been revealed to him by the Holy Spirit that he would not see death before he had seen the Lord's Christ. ²⁷And he came in the Spirit into the temple; and when the parents brought in the child Jesus, to carry out for Him the custom of the Law, ²⁸then he took Him into his arms, and blessed God, and said, ²⁹"Now Lord, You are releasing Your bond-servant to depart in peace, According to Your word; ³⁰For my eyes have seen Your salvation, ³¹Which You have prepared in the presence of all peoples, ³²A Light of revelation to the Gentiles, And the glory of Your people Israel."

ACTS 1:8

[handwritten: last earthly words of Jesus]

". . . but you will receive power when the Holy Spirit has come upon you; and you shall be My witnesses both in Jerusalem, and in all Judea and Samaria, and even to the remotest part of the earth."

ROMANS 10:12–13

¹²For there is no distinction between Jew and Greek; for the same Lord is Lord of all, abounding in riches for all who call on Him; ¹³for "Whoever will call on the name of the Lord will be saved.

God's Universal Purpose Declared (Genesis 12:1–3)

Lesson three explored the turning point of Abraham's calling to go to the Promised Land. God chose Abraham and promised great things: land, a great nation, and blessing. Abraham also had a purpose in this calling—an election for God's mission. We can further explore this event from the perspective of God's ultimate goal in calling Abraham, revealed in the last clause of verse 3: "And in you *all* the families of the earth will be blessed" (Genesis 12:3b, italics added for emphasis). The language is unambiguous. God did not have in mind blessings reserved solely for Israel. God's desire was that *all* families of the earth would experience his blessings.

This fact is crucial for God's people, both then and now, to remember. Our status as God's people is not for our benefit. We are God's people to be about God's mission that *all* would know God.

Emaciated Dreams and an Internal Focus (Isaiah 49:5–6; Luke 2:25–32)

One reason we fail to fully engage in God's mission is our failure in imagination. Our selfish nature leads us to spend our energy and resources taking care of our personal desires and needs or the desires of our immediate family. Collectively, our churches often spend our time and resources internally, and our goal simply becomes self-preservation or keeping the institution going. God has something larger in mind for us!

An Old Testament Version: Isaiah 49:5–6. The setting for this chapter in Isaiah is the same as the Isaiah passage treated in lesson one. Briefly put, Isaiah was speaking with regard to one of Israel's lowest points, the Babylonian Exile (587–538 B.C.). The surviving portion of Israel, the Southern kingdom of Judah, had been conquered. The Babylonians swept away the crucial landmarks for Jewish life: Jerusalem, the temple, and the ark. The leaders of the Hebrews were taken in captivity to Babylon. As mentioned in lesson one, this certainly appeared to be the end for the Jewish people and for the worship of Yahweh.

God had other plans, however, and in Isaiah, Jeremiah, and Daniel we find the continuing life of the Hebrew people worshiping God in

Babylon. Like anyone living within a culture of different values and different gods, the Jewish people struggled to remain faithful. Lesson one describes their temptation toward joining in the widespread practice of idolatry. Daniel and his friends struggled against such false worship and experienced persecution, facing the fiery furnace (Daniel 3) and the lion's den (Daniel 6).

In this context, Isaiah has pointed out the folly of following in idolatry (Isaiah 44—46). Isaiah 47 turns to the arrogant Babylonians with the Lord's message. The victory of the Babylonians over Israel was not a testimony to their strength or strategies. God, rather, used Babylon as a tool of judgment on his disobedient people. Babylon's domination would not last. Isaiah 48 proclaims the coming deliverance for Israel in spite of Israel's failure to keep the covenant and remain faithful to God.

The means of this salvation comes in Isaiah 49: God's Servant. This section of Isaiah contains four "Servant songs," describing God's Servant

ROGER WILLIAMS

Roger Williams organized the first Baptist church in the New World in Providence, Rhode Island, in 1639. He had sought to escape religious persecution in England by traveling to Boston in 1631. He quickly faced opposition and persecution and moved to Plymouth, where he lived, farming and preaching, from 1631–1633. It was in Plymouth that he sensed God's calling to a significant *they/them* for the seventeenth-century colonists—Native Americans. Williams learned several of their languages and worked diligently among them, preaching to them and advocating for them. Leon McBeth commented, "No leader in early America was more influential among the Indians, or more trusted by them, than Roger Williams."[3]

In 1633, the religious authorities harassed Williams again, and he returned to Boston. There he faced challenges from a religious court for his teachings. Williams was advocating strongly for both the separation of church and state and for the rights of Native Americans. Williams learned of his imminent arrest for deportation to England in January of 1636, and he fled into the wilderness. His ministry to Native Americans saved his life, for they sheltered him through the bitter winter. Williams clearly saw the implications of the gospel for a people too often viewed as enemies.

for achieving deliverance and salvation. These passages are 42:1–9; 49:1–6; 50:4–9; and 52:13—53:12. Bible scholars have long debated the identity of this Servant. Some have suggested it was Cyrus, the ruler of Persia, who would conquer the Babylonians and allow the Jews to return to the Promised Land. Others have claimed the Servant was Israel as a whole. While we cannot be sure how people in Isaiah's day interpreted this figure, we find here the clearest Old Testament depiction of Christ. This Servant would be what Israel never could—obedient to God and faithfully showing God's glory to others.[1]

Isaiah 49:5–6 contains a remarkable twist regarding the task of the Servant. What would a defeated people living in exile in the midst of a seemingly impregnable empire dream about? As they sat around the glowing embers of the fire and shared stories of the old days, what did they dare to express, hoping against hope? The optimistic ones might talk about managing to continue as a people while in Babylon. The wildly improbable hope was returning to the Promised Land with their own fields, vineyards, temple, and capital of Jerusalem.

The Servant, however, hears an even greater dream from God. It is "too small a thing" to return and rebuild (Isa. 49:6). God takes their wildest dreams and shows them to be totally inadequate compared to his plans for them. God did not want them to just return to the *good ol' days*. The truth was that in the best of days they rarely maintained their part of God's covenant. God's greater dream was to move them beyond themselves that they would be "a light of the nations so that My salvation may reach to the end of the earth" (49:6). That is a God-sized dream!

A New Testament Version: Luke 2:25–32. We find a comparable recasting of dreams in the birth account of Jesus in Luke 2. After the

EMBRACING *THEY/THEM*

- List those groups or nationalities that may be scorned by many in the church or by our wider culture.
- Identify ways the gospel could connect to their culture or people.
- Use your gifts, contacts, or resources to show God's love.

Bethlehem manger (Luke 2:7), the heavenly host (2:13–14), and the visit of the shepherds (2:15–16), Mary and Joseph took Jesus to the temple to offer the appropriate sacrifices. According to the law, this ritual was to take place after forty days. In the midst of carrying out this ceremony, the family encountered a most remarkable man. Scripture honors few people with descriptions like Simeon's: "This man was righteous and devout, looking for the consolation of Israel; and the Holy Spirit was upon him" (2:25). We might read the description of the shepherds in the Christmas story as referring to ordinary people who respond to news of the birth of Jesus. Simeon, however, represents the best of Old Testament faith. His life was one of quiet trust in God. He had waited his whole life, for he knew that God had acted in the past and would act again. God had revealed in some way at some point that he would live to see the Christ. Simeon is therefore the one person in the story ready and waiting for this very moment.

Simeon's sensitivity to the Spirit's prompting shines through again in being led to the temple at this moment. He took the child in his arms and immediately realized the fulfillment of his life's waiting. What he discovered appears to be different from his expectations. Simeon was "looking for the consolation of Israel." Some scholars have seen a continuation of the feeling of Exile in first-century Judaism.[2] While the people were back in the land with a rebuilt temple and Jerusalem, they were living under Roman domination and taxation. Many expected the Messiah to rectify this situation and free the people. Simeon's expectation of Israel's "consolation" may have been along those lines. What he actually found or sensed in Jesus was something different and greater: "For my eyes have seen your salvation, Which you have prepared in the presence of *all* peoples, a light of revelation *to the Gentiles*, and the glory of Your people Israel" (2:30–32, italics added for emphasis). Simeon saw in the six-week-old eyes of Jesus the fulfillment of that original promise to Abraham for *all* nations.

Shockwaves of God's Purpose (Acts 1:8)

The Book of Acts records the progress of God's universal plan. Luke's first volume, the Gospel of Luke, traced the movement of Jesus and the disciples on the journey toward Jerusalem and the cross. Luke's second volume, Acts, follows the movement of the good news away from Jerusalem, shattering ancient barriers as it goes.

Acts opens with the disciples in Jerusalem, waiting for instructions. In 1:6, they asked the risen Lord whether the blessings *for Israel* were at hand: "Is it at this time You are restoring the kingdom to Israel?" Jesus responded that matters of timing belong to God alone. The disciples' role comes in verse 8, to "be My witnesses." Jesus' aim surpassed "restoration" for Israel. Jesus' desire was that the disciples would cross the deep and bitter divides of Jew/Samaritan and Jew/Gentile. God's promise for blessings to all nations spread like cross-cultural shockwaves from the epicenter of Jerusalem.

A Theology of Salvation Open to All (Romans 10:12–13)

It is fitting that Paul, the apostle to the Gentiles, pronounced the logical conclusion to God's universal designs. The entire history of Israel expressed their struggle to be distinct from others. The dietary laws and circumcision were two expressions of such distinctiveness. In Romans 10, however, Paul proclaimed with directness and clarity God's openness to all.

In a section of Romans beginning in chapter 9, Paul reflected on the rejection of the Messiah by so many of his people, Israel. Paul went so far as to proclaim, "I could wish that I myself were accursed, separated from Christ for the sake of my brethren [Israel]" (Romans 9:3). At the same time he celebrated the surprise of the Gentile response to the gospel. The possibility of this surprising turn of events hung on God's gracious offer of salvation through faith. Instead of salvation coming from circumcision, keeping the law, or having the right parentage or nationality, salvation comes "if you confess with your mouth Jesus as Lord, and believe in your heart that God raised Him from the dead" (Rom. 10:9).

In 10:12–13 Paul took this to its logical (although still scandalous) conclusion, that the Jew/Gentile distinction had been dissolved. God's original plan with Abraham has reached the period of fulfillment in the work of Christ. Now, "*whoever* will call on the name of the Lord will be saved" (10:13, italics added for emphasis).

LESSON 4: *The Mission's Unlimited Reach*

The Universal Mission for Us

God's desires are clear. God wants all people to know him, and God wants his people to be witnesses to others. This is where our pronouns are so important. The most fundamental *we/us* in our lives should be the body of God's people around the world. We share with them our most fundamental task of bearing witness to Christ. As a result, we have more in common with the believing Nigerian villager than with our unbelieving next-door neighbors.

Given God's desires that all know him, we must evaluate our actions and attitudes toward all of the *they/them's* around us. *They* may be from another country. *They* may have different political leanings. *They* may be regarded by our government as *illegal*. *They* may practice lifestyles different from ours. No matter who *they* are, we know how God feels about them. God wants them to know him, and he wants us to be his witnesses for that purpose.

QUESTIONS

1. Who are some groups of people in your community who need to hear the message of the gospel?

2. How has God equipped you to be his witnesses with some of them?

3. How are your goals focused on yourself and your family? How are they focused on the purposes of God?

NOTES

1. John N. Oswalt, *The Book of Isaiah: Chapters 40–66*, The New International Commentary on the Old Testament (Grand Rapids, Michigan: Eerdmans Publishing Company, 1998), 291.

2. N.T. Wright, *The Challenge of Jesus: Rediscovering Who Jesus Really Was and Is* (Downers Grove, Illinois: InterVarsity Press, 1999), 29.

3. H. Leon McBeth, *The Baptist Heritage* (Nashville, TN: Broadman Press, 1987), 133.

UNIT TWO
What God's Mission Is About

The three lessons in this unit focus on what God's mission is about. They show that God is concerned about both spiritual and physical needs and that this same fullness of concern is seen in Jesus, who embodies God's mission.

Sometimes Christians have emphasized one set of needs or the other—spiritual or physical—but not both. Sometimes we have given lip service to one or the other and actually neglected both areas in practice. Let these lessons remind us of the fullness of God's mission—concern for both physical and spiritual needs—and lead us to decide on ways we will participate in all of it.[1]

UNIT TWO. WHAT GOD'S MISSION IS ABOUT

Lesson 5	God's Mission: Redemption and Reconciliation	Exodus 5:22—6:8; 15:1–2, 13; Isaiah 55:6–7; Colossians 1:13–14; Hebrews 9:11–14
Lesson 6	God's Mission: Restoration and Justice	Deuteronomy 15:1–11; Micah 6:8; Jeremiah 7:1–7; Luke 4:16–21; James 1:27; 2:14–16
Lesson 7	God's Mission: Embodied in Jesus	Matthew 11:2–6; 23:23–24; John 1:10–14; Romans 3:21–26; Philippians 2:9–11

NOTES

1. Unless otherwise indicated, all Scripture quotations in unit 2, lessons 5–7, are from the New Revised Standard Version Bible.

FOCAL TEXTS
Exodus 5:22—6:8; 15:1–2, 13;
Isaiah 55:6–7;
Colossians 1:13–14;
Hebrews 9:11–14

BACKGROUND
Exodus 5:22—6:8;
15:1–21; Isaiah 55; Mark
10:45; Colossians 1:9–14;
Hebrews 9:1—10:18

MAIN IDEA
God's mission is to provide a way for all people to live fully in right relationship to him.

QUESTION TO EXPLORE
In what ways are we participating in God's mission to offer redemption and reconciliation to people?

STUDY AIM
To identify ways I will participate in God's mission of offering redemption and reconciliation to people

QUICK READ
God seeks to redeem people from all that enslaves them and to restore them to right relationship with him

LESSON FIVE
God's Mission: Redemption and Reconciliation

How big is your vision of God? Sadly, too often our actions as churches seem rather small when contrasted to the greatness of God, especially as revealed in the cross of Christ.

Take, for example, the church that recently held a lottery for new visitors. The idea was that first-time visitors would be eligible for a drawing for two $500 gasoline cards. The gimmick reminded me of how stores advertise sale items to try to get people to come and buy from them. But what does a drawing for gas cards have to do with the cross of Christ or Christ's calling to take up our crosses and follow him? Of course, the idea was to *get folks in the store.* Yet, such *inch-deep, mile-wide* theology rarely if ever moves people to the point of life-sustaining, substantive faith that propels them to be the incarnation of God.

A shallow theology born of a weak vision seldom leads to a view with more substance to it. The old adage, "you get what you pay for," is relevant. As someone has wisely observed, "What you win them with is what you win them to!" A shallow theology may be easy, but cheap grace is neither sustaining nor life-engaging. To me, the greatest threat to the church is not atheism but *shallowism,* which has all the substance of cotton candy.

So, what might a vision worthy of God look like? To get at this question, let me ask another. More than any other, what place on earth most inspires your soul? If you could travel only to one spot, where would you go? Perhaps the immediate response is, *Do I have to choose? Can't I list multiple places?*

As a resident of Georgia, if I had to choose one spot that stirs my soul more than any other, one place whose vista inspires me, it would be the view from atop Georgia's highest mountain, Brasstown Bald. (As I think about the view from this mountain, you may want to think about your own inspiring view.)

The Cherokee Indians referred to what we call Brasstown Bald as *the place of fresh green.* Indeed, its lush vegetation is as beautiful as the vista afforded when climbing to the top of the mountain. When one gets to the top, one can see for miles in every direction. A sign atop the mountain testifies that you can see four different states. Honestly, though, I can't see the state boundary lines, where one state boundary ends and another begins. I can't see any limits at all save that of the grandeur of the vast horizon. What I can see is the infinite beauty of God's love revealed in his creation.

As one ascends to the top, one notices the ancient oaks whose limbs have been twisted into their strange shape by the power of constant winds. The scene reminds me of the Olive Garden Series by Vincent Van Gogh. A friend of Van Gogh's had painted a statue of Christ with a calm expression and a flowing robe. The statue stands in the midst of an olive garden. The intent was to render a scene of calm and comfort. The painting incensed Van Gogh to the point that he was motivated to paint the Olive Garden Series. Like the contorted oak limbs atop Brasstown Bald, Van Gogh's late nineteenth-century Olive Garden Series portrays Christ in the twisted limbs themselves, without Christ's statue set in stone.[1]

I think Van Gogh was onto something. The winds do shape us. In the midst of life's gnarling storms, though, God in Christ is not about just *getting us in the door* of salvation. In Christ, rather, we are redeemed, and in the redemption we are called into a life of service that heralds Christ's good news. Such a vision of God and of the servants who follow him as Lord is a testimony to the wonder of the cross and its transformative power. This is the vision we must both experience and share.

EXODUS 5:22—6:8

²²Then Moses turned again to the LORD and said, "O LORD, why have you mistreated this people? Why did you ever send me? ²³Since I first came to Pharaoh to speak in your name, he has mistreated this people, and you have done nothing at all to deliver your people." ⁶:¹Then the LORD said to Moses, "Now you shall see what I will do to Pharaoh: Indeed, by a mighty hand he will let them go; by a mighty hand he will drive them out of his land." ²God also spoke to Moses and said to him: "I am the LORD. ³I appeared to Abraham, Isaac, and Jacob as God Almighty, but by my name "The LORD' I did not make myself known to them. ⁴I also established my covenant with them, to give them the land of Canaan, the land in which they resided as aliens. ⁵I have also heard the groaning of the Israelites whom the Egyptians are holding as slaves, and I have remembered my covenant. ⁶Say therefore to the Israelites, "I am the LORD, and I will free you from the burdens of the Egyptians and deliver you from slavery to them. I will redeem

you with an outstretched arm and with mighty acts of judgment. ⁷I will take you as my people, and I will be your God. You shall know that I am the Lord your God, who has freed you from the burdens of the Egyptians. ⁸I will bring you into the land that I swore to give to Abraham, Isaac, and Jacob; I will give it to you for a possession. I am the Lord.'"

Exodus 15:1–2, 13

¹Then Moses and the Israelites sang this song to the Lord: ""I will sing to the Lord, for he has triumphed gloriously; horse and rider he has thrown into the sea. ²The Lord is my strength and my might, and he has become my salvation; this is my God, and I will praise him, my father's God, and I will exalt him.

. . . .

¹³ "In your steadfast love you led the people whom you redeemed; you guided them by your strength to your holy abode.

Isaiah 55:6–7

⁶Seek the Lord while he may be found, call upon him while he is near; ⁷let the wicked forsake their way, and the unrighteous their thoughts; let them return to the Lord, that he may have mercy on them, and to our God, for he will abundantly pardon.

Mark 10:45

For the Son of Man came not to be served but to serve, and to give his life a ransom for many.

Colossians 1:13–14

¹³ He has rescued us from the power of darkness and transferred us into the kingdom of his beloved Son, ¹⁴ in whom we have redemption, the forgiveness of sins.

LESSON 5: *God's Mission: Redemption and Reconciliation*

HEBREWS 9:11–14

¹¹But when Christ came as a high priest of the good things that have come, then through the greater and perfect tent (not made with hands, that is, not of this creation), ¹²he entered once for all into the Holy Place, not with the blood of goats and calves, but with his own blood, thus obtaining eternal redemption. ¹³For if the blood of goats and bulls, with the sprinkling of the ashes of a heifer, sanctifies those who have been defiled so that their flesh is purified, ¹⁴how much more will the blood of Christ, who through the eternal Spirit offered himself without blemish to God, purify our conscience from dead works to worship the living God!

A Promise of Redemption (Exodus 5:22—6:8)

The promise of redemption is all-encompassing and emphasizes God's commitment both to individuals and to the larger community. Exodus 5:22—6:8 shows God in the act of preparing to redeem God's people from Egyptian bondage. The promise that Moses was to convey to the people is but another stanza of God's eternal covenant of love.

Four times in this passage (Exodus 6:2, 6, 7, 8), God pronounced "I am the LORD." The central point of the Exodus drama is not the Hebrew people. It's not the Pharaoh, either. Rather, the central point is that God who has always been known as the all-powerful one now reveals himself as the personal Lord. He heard the groaning of his people and in response, chose to establish a covenant of love (Exod. 2:24–25; 6:2). The text in essence says, *It's one thing to know my power; it's a new and wonderful thing to know me as Lord.* God asserts, "I will take you as my people, and I will be your God. You shall know that I am the LORD your God . . ." (Exod. 6:7).

The Promise Fulfilled (Exodus 15:1–2, 13)

God soon fulfilled the promise of redemption that he made to Moses and through Moses to the people. After God had brought them safely across the sea and destroyed Pharaoh's army, Moses and the Israelites could not help but sing, "The LORD is my strength and my might, and he has become my salvation; this is my God, and I will praise him ..." (Exod. 15:2). Such is the affirmation of those who have experienced God's redemption.

Each of us finds ourselves at times under the oppression of Pharaoh in a distant and foreign land. Perhaps the oppression is chronic in nature, such as a disease we cannot control or a pain we cannot ease. Maybe the fear of the unknown or a future we can't control is the burden of the Pharaoh's power. Maybe Egypt is a marriage or a relationship with children that we are struggling to manage and with which we find ourselves barely able to cope. It may be a job we cannot stand or pressures and stresses that do not seem to let up.

Yes, Egypt's oppression comes in a myriad of forms, as does the wandering in the wilderness that always seems to accompany it. Even so, that which was true of old is true today. The all-powerful God of Abraham and Sarah, Isaac and Rebekah, and Jacob and Rachel has come to us as Lord. He yearns to redeem each of us. He loves us, and he calls us into the light of love.

But God's vision is bigger than any one of us. Our Western worldview and its emphasis on the individual has fed this understanding. Yet, in the Exodus affirmation of God's redeeming work, we see that God's redemption is for the community of Hebrew people.[2] Acceptance of the communal aspect of salvation remains one of the greatest challenges for the church. God has saved us to love others.

A Vision of Relationship with God (Isaiah 55:6–7)

Do we readily see the vision God intends? The prophet Isaiah asked, "Why do you spend your money for that which is not bread, and your labor for that which does not satisfy?" (Isaiah 55:2). He then pleaded, "Seek the LORD while he may be found, call upon him while he his near" (Isa. 55:6).

There was a sense of urgency in the prophet's voice about the need for God's presence as the foundation for life. The gift of relationship with the divine was everything. In an age that has allowed materialism to become the new Promised Land, the prophet's word is a challenge to our priorities.

Jesus' Redemptive Work (Mark 10:45; Colossians 1:13–14; Hebrews 9:11–14)

God's redemptive work as described in the Old Testament provides the backdrop for the focus on God's redemptive work through Jesus in the New Testament. Consider these three rich texts in the New Testament about Jesus' redemptive work.

Mark 10:45 expresses a great truth in a pointed way. This verse speaks the language of redemption as Jesus expressed the intent of his life—"not to be served but to serve, and to give his life a ransom for many." There's no shallow theology here. Rather what we see is the depth of our need—we were enslaved and needed to be freed—and the extent to which Jesus would go to redeem us—"give his life."

Colossians 1:13–14 is part of Paul's emphasis in the Letter to the Colossians on the grandeur of what Christ has done for us. As with Mark 10:45 and, indeed, each of the texts previously studied in this lesson, we see both our great need—"rescued us from the power of darkness"—and the greatness of what God has done for us in Christ—"transferred us into the kingdom of his beloved Son, in whom we have redemption, the forgiveness of sins."

Hebrews 9:11–14 pictures Christ's redemptive work in comparison to the sacrificial system of Old Testament days. The Old Testament sacrifices had to be repeated. Christ's sacrifice was "once for all." Infinitely more impressive, the Old Testament sacrifices were "the blood of goats and calves," but Christ's sacrifice was of himself, "his own blood, thus obtaining eternal redemption." Should we not be singing now, just as Moses and the Israelites did after God's redemption from Egypt?

Conclusion

What about you and me? In our effort to discern the vastness of God's mercy and the wideness of God's love, how is it that we let Egypt get in the way? So I must ask myself, *Where are the places in my life that I am driven toward some other end than the love of God?*

Ambition; political divisions; theological divisions; arrogance; insecurity; self-righteousness; racial and class divisions; hurts we have experienced from other people; and the sheer power of materialism—all of these and more can be the Pharaoh in our midst. That which binds and controls us can in fact keep us from crossing the Red Sea with God and marching onward toward the Promised Land.

In the midst of his own wilderness journey, Jesus had every opportunity to succumb to the economic, political, and religious temptations of his day. He refused, though, the choice of selfish dominance, envisioning instead God's kingdom of love. Quoting the prophet Isaiah, Jesus said (Luke 4:18-19):

> The Spirit of the Lord is upon me,
>   because he has anointed me
>   to bring good news to the poor.
> He has sent me to proclaim release to the captives
>   and recovery of sight to the blind,
>   to let the oppressed go free,
>   to proclaim the year of the Lord's favor.

The Message paraphrases that last line like this: "This is God's year to act!" So this is a big vision! And this vision—God's vision—is a vision to which we are called to respond and to share.

How big is our vision? The call through Moses of old to the oppressor to let my people go was fully realized in the fullness of God in Christ. He came not to serve but to give his life in order to free all—including you and me—from that which binds us.

To me, giving gas cards away seems comical but also sad. It's sad that the church would feel the need to attract people with something other than the merits of God's love and sad that people would be motivated by such rather than by the freedom and peace that Christ alone affords.

There should be no need for gimmicks because God's vision of love is compelling and contagious in and of itself. Those who feel it, experience it, and are called by it know that they cannot keep from singing. Those motivated by it cannot help but serve God with all their hearts, souls, minds, and being because they have been released from the oppression of Egypt.

UNDERSTANDING HONOR IN THE BIBLICAL TRADITION

God's promise of redemption made to Israel through Moses suggests an understanding of God as that of a strong kinsman whose role it is to restore the honor of the family by protecting it against injustice, poverty, and threat.[3] The biblical portrait depicts God as one who is involved in protecting his family against all manner of harm.[4]

Thus, very early in the biblical drama, God is understood as protector. This dynamic awareness would pave the way for the work of Christ and for our calling as we participate in God's mission.

The vision of the Exodus drama in which God promised to redeem his people must be understood over against the political, economic, social, and spiritual injustices at hand. Look at the burdens described in Exodus 1. The Hebrews were forced by a pharaoh who did not know the covenant God to build cities and toil in the fields. Their lives were made bitter under the ruthless hand of Egypt's vision—a vision built on the power of self-aggrandizement.

But as the strong kinsman, God redeemed his people. God was willing to address the *political* tyranny of the Pharaoh. His call to let his people go was understood as a divine intervention in the face of *economic* injustices and exploitation by the Egyptian nation for its own agricultural and construction ends. God was also willing to work in the hearts of people on their behalf. Pharaoh had ordered all the Hebrew male babies to be killed, but the stirring of God's love in the hearts of Egyptian midwives prevented this from happening. Too, the Hebrews believed the hand of God had been raised on their behalf with the consequence that *social* genocide was prevented.

Why did God invest himself in the Hebrew's political, economic, and social trauma? Because there were *spiritual* consequences at play. This is the central story of God's vision then and now. The Hebrews' slavery kept them from knowing fully the freeing love of God.[5]

QUESTIONS

1. Consider the statement, "What you win them with is what you win them to." What do you think this observation means? What, if any, is the relevance for understanding and committing to God's mission of redemption and reconciliation?

2. What are some ways in which we can share the good news of God's redemption so that people are truly won to the Christ who calls us to follow him?

3. Do you feel that God's mission of redemption is strictly spiritual in nature or that it has social and physical concerns as well?

4. How might the biblical image of redemption from Egypt be a symbol for our time?

NOTES

1. Jeff Dugan, Vincent van Gogh. "Olive Grove and Olive Grove, Orange Sky." http://arttoheartweb.com/worshipresources/offertories/offvanGoghOlive.htm. Accessed 1/29/09.
2. Christopher J.H. Wright, *The Mission of God: Unlocking the Bible's Grand Narrative* (Downers Grove, Illinois: IVP Academic, 2006), 265–288.
3. Wright, *The Mission of God*, 266.
4. Wright, *The Mission of God*, 267.
5. Wright, *The Mission of God*, 268–272.

LESSON SIX
God's Mission: Restoration and Justice

FOCAL TEXTS
Deuteronomy 15:1–11; Micah 6:8; Jeremiah 7:1–7; Luke 4:16–21; James 1:27; 2:14–16

BACKGROUND
Deuteronomy 15:1–11; Leviticus 25; Isaiah 61:1–3; Jeremiah 7:1–15; Micah 6:6–8; Luke 4:14–30; James 1:27—2:17

MAIN IDEA
God's mission is to bring restoration and justice to people who are needy and oppressed.

QUESTION TO EXPLORE
Does God care about people who are needy and oppressed?

STUDY AIM
To identify ways I will participate in God's mission of offering restoration and justice to people

QUICK READ
Seeking the heart of Christ means that we are to desire to be Christ's hands in a hurting world. God is concerned about people's physical needs as well as their spiritual needs.

What do you do when there are not enough good things to go around? The bumper sticker theology, "he who has the most toys wins," is one response. Perhaps you remember the schoolyard game, *king of the hill*. There the idea was to conquer the top of the hill. If you were the person fortunate to get to the top, the object of the game was to keep others from getting there. You had to claw your way to the top, pushing others away, and you had to bring down others who were ahead of you. As a childhood game, it was a lot of fun, but in the game of life, the quest to be king of the hill can be unhealthy because it is contrary to God's way.

The biblical drama, though, affirms the abundance of God and God's overwhelming generosity. It celebrates trust in God and shuns anxiety. In the Bible, creation is portrayed as a dance of beauty and balance that calls forth the freedom of abandoning oneself to the goodness of God's care and perfect order for life.[1] But such was not to continue. Balanced order in the Garden of Eden gave way to a pursuit of the "tree of knowledge of good and evil" (Genesis 2:17). Care for each other was replaced with Cain's haunting response to God, "am I my brother's keeper?" (Gen. 4:9).[2]

Cain's question is as old as existence itself. Wanting to have the power of God, desiring to be the creator of our own destiny, and caring only for self—such a lifestyle has consequences that have resulted in an imbalance both within our own lives and in the larger world community. Jealousy, greed, insecurity, arrogance, and ignorance are all a part of the imbalance. Wealth in the hands of a limited few is also a part of the imbalance.

So what are people of faith to do? We are called by God to look at the imbalance; to consider our contributions to its cause; and to hear again the powerful call of Scripture not only for redemption but also for restoration and justice.

DEUTERONOMY 15:1–11

[1]Every seventh year you shall grant a remission of debts. [2]And this is the manner of the remission: every creditor shall remit the claim that is held against a neighbor, not exacting it of a neighbor who is a member of the community, because the LORD's remission has been proclaimed. [3]Of a foreigner you may exact it, but you

must remit your claim on whatever any member of your community owes you. ⁴There will, however, be no one in need among you, because the LORD is sure to bless you in the land that the LORD your God is giving you as a possession to occupy, ⁵if only you will obey the LORD your God by diligently observing this entire commandment that I command you today. ⁶When the LORD your God has blessed you, as he promised you, you will lend to many nations, but you will not borrow; you will rule over many nations, but they will not rule over you. ⁷If there is among you anyone in need, a member of your community in any of your towns within the land that the LORD your God is giving you, do not be hardhearted or tight-fisted toward your needy neighbor. ⁸You should rather open your hand, willingly lending enough to meet the need, whatever it may be. ⁹Be careful that you do not entertain a mean thought, thinking, "The seventh year, the year of remission, is near," and therefore view your needy neighbor with hostility and give nothing; your neighbor might cry to the LORD against you, and you would incur guilt. ¹⁰Give liberally and be ungrudging when you do so, for on this account the LORD your God will bless you in all your work and in all that you undertake. ¹¹Since there will never cease to be some in need on the earth, I therefore command you, "Open your hand to the poor and needy neighbor in your land."

MICAH 6:8

He has told you, O mortal, what is good; and what does the LORD require of you but to do justice, and to love kindness, and to walk humbly with your God?

JEREMIAH 7:1–7

¹The word that came to Jeremiah from the LORD: ²Stand in the gate of the LORD's house, and proclaim there this word, and say, Hear the word of the LORD, all you people of Judah, you that enter these gates to worship the LORD. ³Thus says the LORD of hosts, the God of Israel: Amend your ways and your doings, and let me dwell with you in this place. ⁴Do not trust in these deceptive words: "This

is the temple of the Lord, the temple of the Lord, the temple of the Lord." ⁵For if you truly amend your ways and your doings, if you truly act justly one with another, ⁶if you do not oppress the alien, the orphan, and the widow, or shed innocent blood in this place, and if you do not go after other gods to your own hurt, ⁷then I will dwell with you in this place, in the land that I gave of old to your ancestors forever and ever.

Luke 4:16–21

¹⁶When he came to Nazareth, where he had been brought up, he went to the synagogue on the sabbath day, as was his custom. He stood up to read, ¹⁷and the scroll of the prophet Isaiah was given to him. He unrolled the scroll and found the place where it was written: ¹⁸"The Spirit of the Lord is upon me, because he has anointed me to bring good news to the poor. He has sent me to proclaim release to the captives and recovery of sight to the blind, to let the oppressed go free, ¹⁹to proclaim the year of the Lord's favor." ²⁰And he rolled up the scroll, gave it back to the attendant, and sat down. The eyes of all in the synagogue were fixed on him. ²¹Then he began to say to them, "Today this scripture has been fulfilled in your hearing.

James 1:27

Religion that is pure and undefiled before God, the Father, is this: to care for orphans and widows in their distress, and to keep oneself unstained by the world.

James 2:14–16

¹⁴What good is it, my brothers and sisters, if you say you have faith but do not have works? Can faith save you? ¹⁵If a brother or sister is naked and lacks daily food, ¹⁶and one of you says to them, "Go in peace; keep warm and eat your fill," and yet you do not supply their bodily needs, what is the good of that?

The Importance of Rest (Deuteronomy 15:1–11)

Deuteronomy 15:1 contains the command that "at the end of every seven years you must cancel debts." Verses 4–5 add, "There will, however, be no one in need among you, because the LORD is sure to bless you in the land that the LORD your God is giving you as a possession to occupy, if only you will obey the LORD your God by diligently observing this entire commandment that I command you today." Verses 7–11 continue to call for generosity, concluding with these words: "I therefore command you, 'Open your hand to the poor and needy neighbor in your land" (Deuteronomy 15:11). Observe carefully that God's blessing was inseparably linked to Israel's generosity, including its faithfulness in canceling debts as commanded.

Leviticus 25 expands on the teaching in this passage. There, the seventh year was not only to be a year of cancelling debts, but it was also to be a year of Sabbath rest.[3] The Hebrews were instructed to let the land lie fallow. They were not to labor but to trust in God for the fruits of the fields. By linking the cancellation of debt to the Sabbath rest, economics and faith were connected. The importance of rest was related to the awareness that God's holiness undergirded all facets of the community. The land was God's. Each life was God's. Too, the Sabbath rest awakened the Hebrews to the truth that they were a people once in bondage who now lived the life of promise. The Sabbath rest opened them to the deeper presence of God in their midst. The Sabbath rest also reminded them that they were indeed their brother's keeper, for as God had given for them, so they were to care for one another.

Is God Serious About This? (Micah 6:8)

Theoretically, this idea of caring for one another sounds good. But practically, is God serious? Are God's notions of fairness something we have to take literally, or is this a part of the biblical canon we can overlook? Micah 6:8, a pivotal text in the Old Testament, leaves no doubt. God is concerned that his people "do justice," "love kindness," and "walk humbly with your God."

The context of this verse leaves no doubt that these words are more than noble sentiments that can safely be ignored. The verses that precede

> ## THE THINGS THAT KILL US
>
> In his book, *Blue Like Jazz*, Donald Miller tells the story of Don Rabbit. It seems that Don Rabbit went to Stumpdown Coffee regularly, every morning in fact. "One morning at Stumpdown, Don Rabbit saw Sexy Carrot. And Don Rabbit decided to chase Sexy Carrot." He chased Carrot everywhere, *everywhere*, including all over America and even to the moon. Don Rabbit was very tired. But Rabbit at last caught Carrot. "And the moral of the story is that if you work hard, stay focused, and never give up, you will eventually get what you want in life. Unfortunately, shortly after this story was told, Don Rabbit choked on the carrot and died. So the second moral of the story is: Sometimes the things we want most in life are the things that will kill us."[6]

this verse provide a vivid reminder that God is concerned that people do more than go to church and practice religious rituals (Micah 6:6–7). The verses that follow condemn the evil accumulation of wealth; dishonest business practices; and deceitful behavior (Micah 6:10–12). These wrongs did not exist only in the days of the eighth-century prophet Micah; they continue today. God is concerned about justice today as he was then.

An Urgent Call (Jeremiah 7:1–15)

Several decades after Micah, the prophet Jeremiah dealt with similar wrongs in Judah toward the end of the fifth century B.C. and into the sixth. The Southern kingdom had not learned anything from the earlier destruction of the Northern kingdom.

So we find God calling and pleading through Jeremiah, ". . . For if you truly amend your ways and your doings, if you truly act justly one with another, if you do not oppress the alien, the orphan, and the widow, or shed innocent blood in this place, and if you do not go after other gods to your own hurt, then I will dwell with you in this place, in the land that I gave of old to your ancestors forever and ever" (Jeremiah 7:5–7). Then we find God asking, "Will you steal, murder, commit adultery, swear falsely, make offerings to Baal, and go after other gods that you have not known, and then come and stand before me in this house, which is called by my name, and say, "We are safe!"—only to go on doing all these abominations? Has this house, which is called by my name, become a den of robbers in your sight?" (Jer. 7:9–10).

The people were trusting in the fact that they maintained the religious ritual and professed to be religious. They even sang, "This is the temple of the LORD, the temple of the LORD, the temple of the LORD" (Jer. 7:4). Not nearly good enough, God said, warning, "I will cast you out of my sight" (Jer. 7:15). God demands justice, not just words.

The Year of the Lord's Favor (Luke 4:16–21)

Jesus highlighted the emphasis on justice in his message early in his ministry in the synagogue at Nazareth, his hometown. The Scripture he read was from Isaiah 61:1–3. Note the connection of that passage to the year of Jubilee described earlier in Leviticus 25:10. From the law in Deuteronomy 15 and Leviticus 25 through the prophet Isaiah (Isaiah 61:1–3) to Jesus himself, God's concern is for justice—for the poor, the captives, the blind, the oppressed.

Do the Right Thing (James 1:27; 2:14–16)

In its simplest context, the Jubilee year referred to in Leviticus, Deuteronomy, Isaiah, and then in Luke is God's way of calling each of us to do the right thing. Further, the Book of James echoes Micah and Jeremiah as it defines true religion. "Religion that is pure and undefiled before God, the Father, is this: to care for orphans and widows in their distress, and to keep oneself unstained by the world" (James 1:27). James states further that true faith takes action to help and doesn't just talk about helping. "If a brother or sister is naked and lacks daily food and one of you says to them, 'Go in peace; keep warm and eat your fill,' and yet you do not supply their bodily needs, what is the good of that?" (James 2:15). With these clear teachings, how can we possibly believe that faith is only about words and not about actions, or only about talking about God and not about taking action to help people in need, as God commands throughout Scripture?.

The Fork in the Road

I finally stumbled on the fork in the road in a museum in Rome, Italy. I was with a group of college students. We had traveled there to study the relationship between religion and art.

Our studies took us to the National Museum of Ancient Art. There hanging side by side on a wall were two of the late Renaissance paintings by Caravaggio. On the left was his painting titled "Narcissus."[7] The painting portrays a young man arrayed in the finest clothes of his day staring at his reflection in a pool of water. On the right was Caravaggio's painting of Saint Francis. He is wearing a tattered robe and kneeling before a cross.[8]

To see the two paintings side by side was breathtaking. As I looked, I thought to myself, *I'm standing at the road's divide.* One road leads to an absorption with self; the other to an absorption with service. This is the choice the biblical teaching of Jubilee demands of each of us as well.

I'm not sure how we ever resolve the demands of the gospel with the world in which we live. Some would take literally Jesus' demand that we sell all we have and give it to the poor. For them, the radical call to follow demands no less (see Mark 10:21).

But perhaps like you, I find myself struggling in the world in which I live to be successful without compromising my faith. At least I think I know untruth when I hear it. I remember a friend once commenting to me, "Haven't you learned by now that it's all about money?" Another said, "If you quit feeding the poor, they will go away." And against such a backdrop of selfishness, I hear the succinct choice of Jesus, who said, "You cannot serve God and wealth" (Matthew 6:24). You cannot serve self and others. You cannot be both *king of the hill* and a follower of the Way.

Implications and Actions

Recently our church engaged in a six-week study of the millennium development goals.[4] These are goals that the nations of the world established in order to focus on the need to eradicate the causes of extreme poverty. We engaged in the study as a group of Christians with the thought that if the nations of the world have made eradicating extreme poverty a goal, then maybe the church ought to consider its calling to do the same. In our study, many of us were overwhelmed by the magnitude of the problem. Consider these facts:

- More than a billion people struggle to live on less than one dollar per day
- More than 800 million people struggle with chronic hunger
- More than 10 million of God's precious children die annually before they reach their fifth birthday
- More than 500,000 women die annually during childbirth due to a lack of appropriate medical care
- More than 2.2 million people die each year from diseases associated with poor water and unsanitary conditions

In such a world, God's call for justice is the reminder that "this is [our] Father's world."[5] All that is belongs to God. The Hebrews of old lived with this knowledge. The land they inhabited was God's land and God's gift for which they were responsible. Because the land was God's, they understood that the wealth or capital that the land represented was ultimately not their possession.

The ancient Hebrews understood that resources were limited. To be wealthy meant that others were poor. To draw from the well of wealth meant there was less for others. The capital that some earned meant that others acquired debt, which is the underlying cause for so much poverty. So, in the year of Jubilee, all land was restored to the original families of each tribe, and all financial obligations were written off so that all would have an opportunity once again to contribute to the economic life and viability of the community.

Such matters are hard things to ponder. We become uncomfortable when we consider them. Most people of faith don't know what to do with these teachings. Yet this much is certain. God's concern for justice, expressed throughout Scripture, is a reminder that beyond the church's evangelistic mission to *bring* Jesus Christ to people is the ethical mission to *be* Jesus Christ to people. Seeking the heart of Christ means that we also desire to be Christ's hands in a hurting world. That we often have not is a source of judgment.

QUESTIONS

1. How seriously should contemporary believers take the biblical concept of the year of Jubiliee?

2. Why do you think most people of faith don't seem to do much about God's concern for justice?

3. How concerned should Christians be about God's concern for justice for the poor and the oppressed?

4. What is your church doing to minister to the needy? Does this take place mainly at Christmas?

NOTES

1. Walter Brueggemann, *The Liturgy of Abundance, The Myth of Scarcity*, www.religion-online.org/showarticle.asp?title=533. Accessed 1/29/09.
2. I have written elsewhere about the dimensions of fallenness in Scripture. See Robert C. Shippey, Jr., *Listening in a Loud World* (Macon: Mercer University Press, 2005).
3. Moreover, *seven* in the biblical tradition symbolizes completeness. Jubilee was considered to be a time in which the cycle was made complete and the intent of God's balance for creation was once again restored.
4. See *The Millennium Development Goals Report 2008,* available at millenniumindicators.un.org/unsd/mdg/Resources/Static/Products/Progress2008/MDGReport2008En.pdf, accessed 1/29/09. For an excellent study of the Millennium Development Goals, see the book by Sabina Alkire and Edmund Newell, *What Can One Person Do?* (New York: Church Press Incorporated, 2005).
5. "This Is My Father's World," words by Maltbie D. Babcock, 1901.
6. Donald Miller, *Blue Like Jazz: Nonreligious Thoughts on Christian Spirituality* (Nashville: Thomas Nelson Publishers, 2003), pp. 64–76.
7. See http://www.trincoll.edu/depts/rome/curriculum/rome341.html. Accessed 2/12/09.
8. See http://www.museumsyndicate.com/item.php?item=16045. Accessed 2/12/09.

FOCAL TEXTS
Matthew 11:2–6; 23:23–24;
John 1:10–14;
Romans 3:21–26;
Philippians 2:9–11

BACKGROUND
Isaiah 45:23; Matthew 11:2–6; 23:1–39; John 1:1–18; Romans 3:21–26; Philippians 2:5–11

MAIN IDEA
Jesus embodies God's mission of redemption and reconciliation, restoration and justice.

QUESTION TO EXPLORE
What do Jesus' life and teachings show us about the full scope of God's mission?

STUDY AIM
To commit myself to follow Jesus as he embodies God's mission, ministering to both physical and spiritual needs

QUICK READ
God's mission of ministering to people's needs—both physical and spiritual—was embodied in Jesus, the Word, whom we are to confess as Lord.

LESSON SEVEN
God's Mission: Embodied in Jesus

On July 4 each year, the city of Atlanta celebrates Independence Day with the running of the Peachtree 10k. In light of a recent book titled *1,000 Places to See or Go Before You Die1* and since I live near Atlanta, I thought to myself, *This is one of those Georgia traditions I've got to experience.*

So I did it. The race was fine. The ride after the race on MARTA (Atlanta's commuter rail system) was anything but.

Imagine 200 people, all of whom have just finished running six miles on July 4 in "Hotlanta," crammed into a train car. On my best days, I am claustrophobic. Put me in an oxygen-deprived space with 199 other sticky bodies, and you have a recipe for disaster.

The train car started spinning. I told somebody I had to sit down. One look at my pale face and they gladly got in a sharing spirit quickly. If it had not been for the kindness of a friend who shared a bottle of Gatorade® and started fanning my face, I think we might have had a situation on our hands.

For too many, life has a similar pattern. We find ourselves in boring ruts; or crammed in boxes; or forced into crowded rooms accompanied by stress, anxiety, doubts, chronic pain, loneliness, and stifling grief. We wonder where the door is. We plead for fresh air. We long for the train that we are on to just stop, and we will get off anywhere. Then we are reminded that the train's destiny is life, and we plead for just a crack in the window, so that we can somehow manage one more day.

MATTHEW 11:2–6

[2] When John heard in prison what the Messiah was doing, he sent word by his disciples [3] and said to him, "Are you the one who is to come, or are we to wait for another?" [4] Jesus answered them, "Go and tell John what you hear and see: [5] the blind receive their sight, the lame walk, the lepers are cleansed, the deaf hear, the dead are raised, and the poor have good news brought to them. [6] And blessed is anyone who takes no offense at me."

MATTHEW 23:23–24

[23] "Woe to you, scribes and Pharisees, hypocrites! For you tithe mint, dill, and cummin, and have neglected the weightier matters

of the law: justice and mercy and faith. It is these you ought to have practiced without neglecting the others. ²⁴You blind guides! You strain out a gnat but swallow a camel!

JOHN 1:10–14

¹⁰He was in the world, and the world came into being through him; yet the world did not know him. ¹¹He came to what was his own, and his own people did not accept him. ¹²But to all who received him, who believed in his name, he gave power to become children of God, ¹³who were born, not of blood or of the will of the flesh or of the will of man, but of God. ¹⁴And the Word became flesh and lived among us, and we have seen his glory, the glory as of a father's only son, full of grace and truth.

ROMANS 3:21–26

²¹But now, apart from law, the righteousness of God has been disclosed, and is attested by the law and the prophets, ²²the righteousness of God through faith in Jesus Christ for all who believe. For there is no distinction, ²³since all have sinned and fall short of the glory of God; ²⁴they are now justified by his grace as a gift, through the redemption that is in Christ Jesus, ²⁵whom God put forward as a sacrifice of atonement by his blood, effective through faith. He did this to show his righteousness, because in his divine forbearance he had passed over the sins previously committed; ²⁶it was to prove at the present time that he himself is righteous and that he justifies the one who has faith in Jesus.

PHILIPPIANS 2:10–11

⁹Therefore God also highly exalted him and gave him the name that is above every name, ¹⁰so that at the name of Jesus every knee should bend, in heaven and on earth and under the earth, ¹¹and every tongue should confess that Jesus Christ is Lord, to the glory of God the Father.

God's Mission of Restoration and Justice in Jesus (Matthew 11:2–6; 23:23–24)

Perhaps something like the experience of my ill-fated train ride is what John the Baptist was feeling when he asked Jesus, "Are you the one who is to come, or are we to wait for another?" (Matthew 11:2). In prison, he must have felt like the walls were caving in on him. Longing for the one whose path he believed he had cleared, John found himself doubting the nature of the master he had chosen to follow. He found himself wondering just what use this Jesus was for his boxed-in condition. After all, why wouldn't Jesus release him from prison, especially since Jesus had promised to set the captives free (see Luke 4:18)? Where was the pending judgment John had thought the Messiah would bring (see Matt. 3:12)?

We do not generally think of John the Baptist as one who doubted. We think of him as the wild man coming out of the desert eating locusts and wild honey. John preferred the feel of camel's hair to the latest in men's apparel. We think of John's voice crying in the wilderness, calling for the crooked paths to be made straight and the mountains to be made low so that all would know the salvation of God soon to be manifest in the person of Jesus (3:1–12). Yet, John now doubted. He questioned. But he was not rebuked.

Jesus simply said, "Blessed is anyone who takes no offense at me" (11:6). Jesus did not reprimand John for doubting or rebuke him for questioning. Jesus simply told those who had come on behalf of John to go back and report what they had seen and heard. Then in case they missed the dynamic acts of grace in their midst, Jesus spelled out what they needed to report: "the blind receive their sight, the lame walk, the lepers are cleansed, the deaf hear, the dead are raised, and the poor have good news brought to them" (11:4–5).

Jesus, in one short command, has summarized all that has happened in the preceding chapters of the Gospel of Matthew. Recall Matthew's emphasis on Jesus' teachings, seen especially in the Sermon on the Mount in Matthew 5—7. But Jesus evidently realized that hearing might not be enough. So Jesus also gave John's followers plenty to report regarding what they had seen (Matt. 8—9). These chapters are filled with Jesus' acts of mercy and restoration. Jesus gave feet to his message. He made people whole.

LESSON 7: *God's Mission: Embodied in Jesus*

Too, had John the Baptist's question about Jesus come later in Jesus' ministry, he might have seen even more clearly Jesus' concern for justice. The Pharisees certainly saw it. Jesus uttered a series of "woes" on the Pharisees for their unjust behavior. Matthew recorded it in chapter 23. Jesus charged them with all manner of evil in spite of the stature they thought they had in the world of religion. Jesus' concern for justice can be seen with clarity in Matthew 23:23–24. He condemned them for neglecting "the weightier matters of the law: justice and mercy and faith" (23:23).

God's Mission of Redemption and Reconciliation in Jesus (John 1:10–14; Romans 3:21–26)

In Jesus we can also see clearly, as John the Baptist wanted to see, the focus of God's mission of redemption and reconciliation being enacted—indeed, incarnated, *enfleshed*—in Jesus. Consider two key passages in the New Testament that demonstrate this truth.

John 1:10–14 summarizes both the dark side and the exceedingly bright side of Jesus' ministry. The dark side is that "the world did not know him . . . and his own people did not accept him" (John 1:10–11). The spectacularly bright side is that "to all who received him, who believed in his name, he gave power to become children of God" (1:12). No longer estranged, people who believe in Jesus receive again the unbroken relationship with God that they need and desire. How can this be? It happens because of the One who "became flesh, and dwelt among us" and whom we believe is "the Word . . . and we saw His glory, glory as of the only begotten from the Father, full of grace and truth" (John 1:14, NASB).

Romans 3:21–26 focuses on God's mission of redemption in Jesus from another angle. In these verses, Paul pointedly emphasized that all human efforts to gain salvation fall short of the goal. God, though, has provided the way in Jesus for people to be "justified by his grace as a gift, through the redemption that is in Christ Jesus, whom God put forward as a sacrifice of atonement by his blood, effective through faith" (Romans 3:24–25).

God's Mission and Jesus' Lordship (Philippians 2:9–11)

Philippians 2:9–11 expresses the result of the fullness of God's mission—justice and restoration, redemption and reconciliation—being embodied in Jesus. As a result of Jesus' humbling himself and becoming "obedient to the point of death—even death on a cross . . . God also highly exalted him and gave him the name that is above every name, so that at the name of Jesus every knee should bend, in heaven and on earth and under the earth, and every tongue confess that Jesus Christ is Lord" (Philippians 2:8–11).

Note that the images of verses 10–11 can be traced to Isaiah 45:23, thus asserting Jesus' place of honor in terms that Isaiah had applied to God himself. Indeed, Jesus, who embodied the fullness of God's mission—justice and restoration, redemption and reconciliation—is Lord!

Implications and Actions

So we pause with John the Baptist to ponder the question, "Are you the one?" (Matt. 11:2). To hear Jesus and to see his actions underlines a deeper question about his mission. Further, to not take offense at or fall away from Jesus is in fact a resolve to participate in the larger work of the cross. To embrace Jesus is to embrace Jesus' mission born of the cross. As the One, Jesus embodied the mission of God, which was to bring about redemption and reconciliation and to establish restoration and justice. Are you ready to call this Jesus *Lord* and follow him?

"The Large Crucifixion"

One of the great paintings of the Reformation era is provided by Matthias von Grünewald (about 1515). The painting is titled "The Large Crucifixion." Grünewald portrays John the Baptist as he stands before the crucified Christ.[2] The Christ is limp. Followers mourn and yet resolve to worship. John stands holding open a Bible that reads, "Behold the Lamb of God who takes away the sins of the world." John's gaze, though, is not at the crucified Christ, but toward the viewer, almost as if he is inviting those inclined to listen to join in the unfolding drama of redemption.

Lean into the picture. Ponder the gaze of John. Listen. You can almost hear John asking the question again, "Are you the one?" This time, though, it is no longer directed to Jesus. The question is directed to you and me. Do you hear it? He's now asking each of us, "Are you the one?" He is asking each of us whether we are willing to take up the cross that wiped away the sins of the world and even now seeks to liberate those still held in sin's sway. He's reminding us that it is in the cross that there is forgiveness, and it is in the cross that there is also liberation and justice from every manner of bondage. Here in the One whose hands are nailed to the cross is the means by which all of creation can be healed.

Paul put it this way: "Who will separate us from the love of Christ? Will hardship, or distress, or persecution, or famine, or nakedness, or peril, or sword? . . . No, in all these things we are more than conquerors through him who loved us. For I am convinced that neither death, nor life, nor angels, nor rulers, nor things present, nor things to come, nor powers, nor height, nor depth, nor anything else in all creation, will be able to separate us from the love of God in Christ Jesus our Lord" (Romans 8:35–39). Paul intended these words about the cross to be a guiding light for people of faith.

In Christ's cross alone is there hope for the upside-down priorities of life, and in Christ's cross alone is there release from injustice and oppression of every kind. He calls us forth to proclaim that Jesus is Lord, and he invites us to join in his good news for every life on earth and for every area of life yet to receive the sweet wonder of God's grace.

QUESTIONS

1. Reflecting on John the Baptist's situation, was it appropriate for him to ask Jesus, "Are you the one?"

2. ==What place, if any, does doubt have in a healthy faith?==

3. What did Jesus mean when he said, "Blessed is anyone who takes no offense at me"?

NOTES

1. Patricia Schultz, *1,000 Places to See Before You Die: a Traveler's Life List* (New York: Workman Publishing Company, 2003).
2. http://www.ibiblio.org/wm/paint/auth/grunewald/crucifixion/. Accessed 1/29/09.

UNIT THREE
God's Call to You

For the believer in Jesus Christ, participation in God's mission is not an option. When you accepted Jesus Christ as your Lord and Savior, you became a participant. You participate as a recipient of God's grace.

The six lessons in this unit focus on God's call to participate in his mission. In these lessons you will discover how your life has significance in the plan of God. Your experience, your personality, and your spiritual gifts make you special. God made you and knows you. No one else is like you. God has a vision and purpose for your life.

You will discover in studying this unit how God wants to transform you and make you an instrument of transformation. You will discover the unique purpose of the church as the body of Christ to accomplish Christ's purposes in you and your fellow believers. You will be challenged to see opportunities God is already placing in your path and will discover how you can make a difference in the world.

Sometimes news reports of world events leave us confused and discouraged. In these lessons you will discover that God is reshaping the world for his purposes. God's purposes will ultimately be accomplished in the earth, and righteousness and justice will prevail. What is most exciting, God wants you to be a part of it![1]

UNIT THREE. GOD'S CALL TO YOU

Lesson 8	Experience God's Good News	Luke 19:1–10; Acts 9:1–9, 19b–22; 16:13–15, 25–34
Lesson 9	Live in Faithfulness to God	Romans 12
Lesson 10	Engage in God's Mission Together	Acts 4:32–35; 2 Corinthians 8:1–9; 1 Corinthians 12:4–13; 1 Peter 2:6–10
Lesson 11	Tell the Good News of Redemption and Reconciliation	2 Corinthians 5:11–21; Colossians 1:24–29

Lesson 12	Minister to People's Physical Needs	Deuteronomy 10:14–19; Amos 5:21–24; Matthew 25:31–46
Lesson 13	Participate in God's Mission to Everyone	Matthew 28:16–20; Acts 11:19–26; Revelation 5:1–10

NOTES

1. Unless otherwise indicated, all Scripture quotations in unit 3, lessons 8–13, are from the New American Standard Bible (1995 edition).

LESSON EIGHT
Experience God's Good News

FOCAL TEXTS
Luke 19:1–10; Acts 9:1–9, 19b–22; 16:13–15, 25–34

BACKGROUND
Luke 19:1–10; Acts 9:1–22; 16:13–34

MAIN IDEA
Participating in God's mission grows naturally and directly out of a genuine experience of God's good news.

QUESTION TO EXPLORE
What does becoming a Christian mean?

STUDY AIM
To recognize that participating in God's mission is the normal outcome of becoming a Christian and to analyze whether I have responded in that way myself

QUICK READ
Some experience a sudden conversion to Christ. For others it is more gradual. But every believer participates in God's mission out of a genuine experience of the good news.

Frank Dang grew up in Communist Vietnam. His father, a medic for South Vietnamese forces during the war, had to escape Vietnam when Frank was eight years old. Rescued at sea, his father was introduced to Christ in a refugee camp and then spent ten years saving money to bring his family to join him in New Orleans.

Frank was eighteen when he first heard the name of Jesus. He says he grew up chanting to Buddha. He knew Buddha wasn't God, but he didn't know who God was. After trusting Christ, he spent two years learning English, was awarded a scholarship to Tulane University, and graduated with high honors in mathematics.

Then he felt God's call to missions and ministered in various countries in the Middle East and Far East. For the last four years we have worked closely together at WorldconneX discovering amazing opportunities that God is creating for missions in the twenty-first century. Frank's participation in missions grew naturally and directly out of his genuine experience of God's good news in Jesus Christ.

LUKE 19:1–10

¹He entered Jericho and was passing through. ²And there was a man called by the name of Zaccheus; he was a chief tax collector and he was rich. ³Zaccheus was trying to see who Jesus was, and was unable because of the crowd, for he was small in stature. ⁴So he ran on ahead and climbed up into a sycamore tree in order to see Him, for He was about to pass through that way. ⁵When Jesus came to the place, He looked up and said to him, "Zaccheus, hurry and come down, for today I must stay at your house." ⁶And he hurried and came down and received Him gladly. ⁷When they saw it, they all began to grumble, saying, "He has gone to be the guest of a man who is a sinner." ⁸Zaccheus stopped and said to the Lord, "Behold, Lord, half of my possessions I will give to the poor, and if I have defrauded anyone of anything, I will give back four times as much." ⁹And Jesus said to him, "Today salvation has come to this house, because he, too, is a son of Abraham. ¹⁰"For the Son of Man has come to seek and to save that which was lost."

ACTS 9:1–9, 19B–22

¹Now Saul, still breathing threats and murder against the disciples of the Lord, went to the high priest, ²and asked for letters from him to the synagogues at Damascus, so that if he found any belonging to the Way, both men and women, he might bring them bound to Jerusalem. ³As he was traveling, it happened that he was approaching Damascus, and suddenly a light from heaven flashed around him; ⁴and he fell to the ground and heard a voice saying to him, "Saul, Saul, why are you persecuting Me?" ⁵And he said, "Who are You, Lord?" And He said, "I am Jesus whom you are persecuting, ⁶but get up and enter the city, and it will be told you what you must do." ⁷The men who traveled with him stood speechless, hearing the voice but seeing no one. ⁸Saul got up from the ground, and though his eyes were open, he could see nothing; and leading him by the hand, they brought him into Damascus. ⁹And he was three days without sight, and neither ate nor drank.

. . . .

¹⁹ᵇNow for several days he was with the disciples who were at Damascus, ²⁰and immediately he began to proclaim Jesus in the synagogues, saying, "He is the Son of God." ²¹All those hearing him continued to be amazed, and were saying, "Is this not he who in Jerusalem destroyed those who called on this name, and who had come here for the purpose of bringing them bound before the chief priests?" ²²But Saul kept increasing in strength and confounding the Jews who lived at Damascus by proving that this Jesus is the Christ.

ACTS 16:13–15, 25–34

¹³And on the Sabbath day we went outside the gate to a riverside, where we were supposing that there would be a place of prayer; and we sat down and began speaking to the women who had assembled. ¹⁴A woman named Lydia, from the city of Thyatira, a seller of purple fabrics, a worshiper of God, was listening; and the Lord opened her heart to respond to the things spoken by

Paul. ¹⁵And when she and her household had been baptized, she urged us, saying, "If you have judged me to be faithful to the Lord, come into my house and stay." And she prevailed upon us.

. . . .

²⁵But about midnight Paul and Silas were praying and singing hymns of praise to God, and the prisoners were listening to them; ²⁶and suddenly there came a great earthquake, so that the foundations of the prison house were shaken; and immediately all the doors were opened and everyone's chains were unfastened. ²⁷When the jailer awoke and saw the prison doors opened, he drew his sword and was about to kill himself, supposing that the prisoners had escaped. ²⁸But Paul cried out with a loud voice, saying, "Do not harm yourself, for we are all here!" ²⁹And he called for lights and rushed in, and trembling with fear he fell down before Paul and Silas, ³⁰and after he brought them out, he said, "Sirs, what must I do to be saved?" ³¹They said, "Believe in the Lord Jesus, and you will be saved, you and your household." ³²And they spoke the word of the Lord to him together with all who were in his house. ³³And he took them that very hour of the night and washed their wounds, and immediately he was baptized, he and all his household. ³⁴And he brought them into his house and set food before them, and rejoiced greatly, having believed in God with his whole household.

A Private Party (Luke 19:1–10)

Jesus' visit to Jericho occurred late in his public ministry, shortly before his triumphal entry into Jerusalem. In a matter of days from this visit Jesus would be crucified.

Jericho is one of the most historic cities on the face of the earth. Many believe it is one of the oldest cities in the world. Some of its original structure dates back more than 7,000, perhaps 9,000, years before Christ.[1] It is perhaps best known for its collapse when Joshua and his army crossed the Jordan into the Promised Land (see Joshua 6). The Jericho of Jesus' day was a prosperous city very near the present site, graced with groves of palm trees.

Zaccheus's home was the last place anyone expected Jesus to visit when Jesus came to Jericho. Zaccheus seems to have grown up in Jericho with a chip on his shoulder. He made up for his short stature and the ridicule he likely received in his youth by becoming a tax collector. Collecting taxes for the Romans made him powerful and prosperous. But it did not make him popular. Tax collectors had a reputation for cheating, and they were viewed as traitors. He had sold out to the Romans, and he padded his pockets with the taxes collected from his own kinsmen. No one wanted anything to do with Zaccheus. No one, that is, except Jesus.

Zaccheus did not expect to be noticed from his perch in the sycamore tree when Jesus passed his way. Zaccheus knew any efforts to press through the crowd with his short stature would be hopeless. The people would shove him to the rear, and he would have no opportunity to see. So he climbed the tree, hoping for a glimpse of the famous rabbi.

No one was more shocked than Zaccheus was when Jesus called his name—and, even more, when Jesus invited himself to Zaccheus's house. As Zaccheus led Jesus away to his home, perhaps he glanced back over his shoulder at the astonished crowd that was murmuring and complaining among themselves about Jesus' decision to visit a tax collector.

Jesus' visit with Zaccheus changed Zaccheus's life. Somehow Zaccheus knew that once he met Jesus he could not continue to live as he had. He

LOTTIE MOON

Charlotte Moon was born in Virginia in 1840.[3] As a teenager, she was a skeptic. She did not trust Christ until she was an eighteen-year-old college student. She was one of the first women to receive a master of arts degree from a southern college. After teaching in girls' schools, she followed Christ's call to become a missionary to China in 1873. Contrary to the cultural restraints for women, she gave herself to fulltime evangelism, winning many to faith in Christ. She died of starvation on Christmas Eve, 1912, having given most of her food to the hungry in China. Multiple thousands would not know Jesus today if Charlotte Moon had not come to faith in Christ and given herself to participate in God's mission.

would give half his possessions to the poor and pay back anyone he had cheated four times the amount. By his actions, Zaccheus immediately joined Jesus on Jesus' mission. His joining Jesus on Jesus' mission was a natural overflow of experiencing the good news Jesus brought into his life. That is why Jesus said, "Today, salvation has come to this house, because he too is a son of Abraham" (Luke 19:10).

A Lightning Bolt from Heaven (Acts 9:1–9, 19b–22)

We know him as the Apostle Paul. But as a youth he was known to his family and friends as Saul. At the time of Jesus' crucifixion, he was probably in his late twenties, a brilliant scholar rising rapidly in the ranks of Jewish politics. He was born a Roman citizen, with all the rights and privileges that implied, and grew up in Tarsus. He was a Jew, a student of Gamaliel, the greatest theologian in Jerusalem, and fluent in both Greek and Hebrew. He was ambitious, zealous, and angry. He had unlimited potential for position and power. But all of that changed on the road between Jerusalem and Damascus.

Accompanied by soldiers who had been assigned to his command, Saul was on his way to arrest and imprison Christians in Damascus. He had already participated in an effective purge of followers of Christ in Jerusalem, including Stephen (see Acts 8:1–3). Saul and his party were traveling along the road in broad daylight when a blinding light struck him to the ground. Saul heard a clearly distinct audible voice speaking to him. The voice identified himself as Jesus and instructed him to enter into Damascus and wait for further instructions. Those who were with Saul heard the sound, but they could not discern the words spoken to him (9:7).

Saul arose, shaken and blind, and was led by his companions into the city. In a flash, Saul's world had been turned upside down. All of his assumptions and ambitions crumbled. For three days he sat in the solitary darkness of a lonely room, refusing to either eat or drink. A stranger came to visit, a local believer, one of those he had vowed to arrest. Saul felt this man's hands touch him and heard him explain what had happened to him. The Lord had chosen him as a special instrument to proclaim the good news to the nations. Only then was Saul able to see again.

Lesson 8: Experience God's Good News

> ### Your Influence on Others for Christ's Sake
>
> 1. Write out your personal testimony using the following outline:
>   a. My life before I trusted Jesus Christ
>   b. How I came to faith in Jesus Christ
>   c. How my life is different since trusting in Jesus Christ
> 2. List your circle of friends and family who are not believers.
> 3. Pray daily for each of these that God will draw them to faith in his Son, Jesus.

Likely there was much that Saul did not understand at that moment. But one thing he did understand "immediately" (9:20). Now that he had received the good news of Christ, he was to tell others. Paul is an example of what appears to have been true of all first-century believers. Once they met Jesus and trusted in him, they naturally became participants in Jesus' mission to redeem the lost.

A Gentle River (Acts 16:13–15)

For some, conversion is a quiet and gentle experience. That's the way it was for Lydia.

Paul and his companions arrived in Philippi with great enthusiasm. They had been seeking God's vision for the next step of their journey. Having been prevented by the Holy Spirit from going to Asia or Bithynia, they came to Troas searching for a definite direction from God. They found their answer in a vision in the night, a man of Macedonia urging them to come to Macedonia (16:6–10). Once they received this vision, they headed west as quickly as possible. Luke wrote, "So putting out to sea from Troas, we ran a straight course to Samothrace, and on the day following to Neapolis; and from there to Philippi" (16:11–12).

Philippi was a major city in Macedonia and a Roman colony. So it was a logical place to set up a base of operations for extending the gospel.

However, once they got to Philippi, they weren't sure exactly where to start. "We were staying in this city for some days" (16:2).

Unlike other cities where Paul had started churches, Philippi did not have a synagogue. So, on the Sabbath, Paul and his companions decided to go out by the river, supposing that any Jews in the city would gather there for worship. They found a group of women who had gathered for prayer in a quiet place by the river. They began to speak with the women.

One of these women, Lydia, was a worshiper of God. This means she was a Gentile convert to Judaism. She had responded to the Scripture and placed her faith in *Yahweh*. But she evidently had not heard about Jesus. When Paul and his companions explained the Messianic prophecies fulfilled in Jesus, God immediately opened her heart, and she believed. Not only did she believe, but also she insisted that Paul and his companions take up lodging in her home.

Lydia's faith affected others. Lydia's "household" also believed. The Greek word used here, *oikos*, means more than a literal house or even a traditional family. The term can include everyone in Lydia's immediate sphere of influence. Lydia was a businesswoman, "a seller of purple fabrics" (Acts 16:14). She had moved to Philippi from Thyatira (Thyatira would be listed as one of the seven churches addressed in Revelation 1:11). She had suppliers of purple fabric, and she had buyers in the marketplace. We don't know whether she had a husband or children. But she had influence. Lydia's sphere of influence became the means by which the church first took root in Philippi.

A Cataclysmic Catastrophe (Acts 16:25–34)

Earthquakes can be terrifying. The quake that struck China in 2008 left thousands dead and injured and millions homeless.[2] The images of mothers and fathers weeping over their children who died in collapsed school buildings were heart-rending. Although the earthquake that struck Philippi when Paul and Silas were prisoners was more limited in destructive power, the terrors of the earthquake were just as real.

Sometimes conversion to Christ comes in the context of catastrophe. That's the way it was for the unnamed jailer who appears in this passage. Perhaps he started his career as a Roman soldier with visions of great

HOUSEHOLDS AND NETWORKS

The Greek word *oikos*, translated "household" (Acts 16:15, 31), is an important word for understanding God's strategy for reaching people. The term is similar to our understanding of *networks* of relationship. We form networks of relationship at home, work, school, and recreation. Our networks of relationship help to define our spheres of influence. Most people choose to attend a church based on relationships with family and friends. The people we will most likely influence to believe in Christ are within these networks. The church Paul started at Philippi grew because of the *oikos* networks of influence that Lydia and the jailer brought with them when they believed.

battles and the thrill of victory. More than likely he had no ambitions to become the jailer in the prison at Philippi. His position as Philippian prison guard may have been more punishment than promotion. Instead of military glory, he spent his days surrounded by the stench of sweating prisoners, who hated and cursed him. But Paul and Silas were different. Of course they would sweat just like the rest. But instead of a curse, they blessed him when he fastened their feet in stocks. And they sang.

When the earthquake ended and the crumbling rock and dust settled, the jailer assumed all the prisoners had escaped. Whether he was overwhelmed with despair or whether it was the dishonor of this ultimate failure, he was ready to end his life. He drew his sword, held the point to his chest, gripped the hilt with both hands, and prepared to plunge the blade into his heart.

A prisoner's voice stopped him. "Do not harm yourself, for we are all here!" (Acts 16:28). The astounding behavior the jailer beheld in Paul and Silas prompted the most important question in the Bible, "Sirs, what must I do to be saved?" (16:30). Paul replied with the most important answer in the Bible: "Believe in the Lord Jesus, and you will be saved" (16:31). Only simple faith in Jesus Christ can transform the human heart and provide the ultimate answers to life's most important question.

Paul added an additional promise: "you and your household" (16:31). The Greek word for "household," *oikos*, is the same term used regarding Lydia (16:15). Again, we don't know what family the Roman soldier might have had. But he had a sphere of influence, including colleagues and friends. Paul's statement does not imply that these were automatically saved because of the Roman soldier's faith. But the faith of the Roman soldier would have an affect on those who knew him so that they would be more likely to trust in Christ as well. In effect both the Roman soldier and Lydia became the first missionaries to Philippi and Macedonia.

Implications and Actions

Every follower of Jesus Christ has a story to tell. Some have dramatic stories of how God delivered them from drugs, alcohol, abusive behavior, addictions, and despair. Others have less dramatic stories, like that of Lydia. But whether we experience a dramatic or a quiet conversion, we all have a story to tell.

In addition, we all have a "household." We might not be married. We might not have children. But we all have an *oikos*, a sphere of influence, those people who know us best. Each of us is a missionary to our own "household." No one else can have the influence we can have in the way we live out the commands of Jesus Christ, in the way we trust him, in the way we are conformed to Christ's image, and in the way we tell the story of how Jesus has made the difference in our lives.

QUESTIONS

1. If you are a believer in Jesus Christ, what were the circumstances surrounding your faith experience with Jesus? Was your experience more like that of Zaccheus, Paul, Lydia, or the jailer?

2. If you are a believer in Jesus Christ, what was your life like before you trusted him by faith?

3. If you are a believer in Jesus Christ, how has your faith in Jesus changed your life?

4. ==With whom have you shared your experience of trusting Christ as your Savior?== With whom could or should you share your experience of trusting Christ as your Savior?

NOTES

1. Jericho. (2009). In *Encyclopædia Britannica*. Accessed 1/22/09, from Encyclopædia Britannica Online: http://www.britannica.com/EBchecked/topic/302707/Jericho
2. See news.bbc.co.uk/2/hi/asia-pacific/7416035.stm. Accessed 1/22/09.
3. See http://www.sbhla.org/biomoon.htm. Accessed 1/22/09. See also www.imb.org/main/give/page.asp?StoryID=5562&LanguageID=1709. Accessed 1/22/09.

LESSON NINE
Live in Faithfulness to God

FOCAL TEXT
Romans 12

BACKGROUND
Romans 12

MAIN IDEA
Participating in God's mission means living in faithfulness to God.

QUESTION TO EXPLORE
To what extent would people who observe your life recognize that you are a Christian?

STUDY AIM
To evaluate my life by the behaviors called for in these verses and decide on at least one action I will take in response

QUICK READ
Followers of Jesus Christ are to live transformed lives so that their attitudes and actions demonstrate kingdom values, values different from the accepted values of the world.

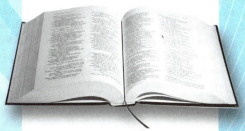

The world was stunned on July 16, 1999, when John F. Kennedy, Jr., his wife Carolyn, and her sister died in the tragic crash of his Piper Saratoga just off the coast of Martha's Vineyard. Investigation of the wreckage confirmed that the aircraft was fully functional when it fell from the skies and plunged into the Atlantic Ocean. The National Transportation Safety Board concluded that Kennedy, piloting his own aircraft, suffered "spatial disorientation."[1] In effect, he thought he was pulling up, when, in reality, he flew the aircraft into a tight death spiral. This is what some call *flying upside down*.

Dallas Willard used this image to introduce the first chapter in his book, *The Divine Conspiracy*.[2] He suggested that most people live without knowing whether they are flying upside down or right-side up. People think they know the rules for survival and order their lives accordingly. But their instincts for self-interest and survival plunge them into a deadly spiral toward disaster. Only Jesus, he concluded, knew how to fly right-side up. This is why Jesus' teachings often seem contradictory to common sense. In Romans 12, the Apostle Paul presented a picture of what flying right-side up looks like.

This chapter introduces the final section of the Book of Romans. This section deals with questions like these: How do you live the Christian life? What does living the Christian life look like?

ROMANS 12

¹Therefore I urge you, brethren, by the mercies of God, to present your bodies a living and holy sacrifice, acceptable to God, which is your spiritual service of worship. ²And do not be conformed to this world, but be transformed by the renewing of your mind, so that you may prove what the will of God is, that which is good and acceptable and perfect. ³For through the grace given to me I say to everyone among you not to think more highly of himself than he ought to think; but to think so as to have sound judgment, as God has allotted to each a measure of faith. ⁴For just as we have many members in one body and all the members do not have the same function, ⁵so we, who are many, are one body in Christ, and individually members one of another. ⁶Since

we have gifts that differ according to the grace given to us, each of us is to exercise them accordingly: if prophecy, according to the proportion of his faith; ⁷if service, in his serving; or he who teaches, in his teaching; ⁸or he who exhorts, in his exhortation; he who gives, with liberality; he who leads, with diligence; he who shows mercy, with cheerfulness. ⁹Let love be without hypocrisy. Abhor what is evil; cling to what is good. ¹⁰Be devoted to one another in brotherly love; give preference to one another in honor; ¹¹not lagging behind in diligence, fervent in spirit, serving the Lord; ¹²rejoicing in hope, persevering in tribulation, devoted to prayer, ¹³contributing to the needs of the saints, practicing hospitality. ¹⁴Bless those who persecute you; bless and do not curse. ¹⁵Rejoice with those who rejoice, and weep with those who weep. ¹⁶Be of the same mind toward one another; do not be haughty in mind, but associate with the lowly. Do not be wise in your own estimation. ¹⁷Never pay back evil for evil to anyone. Respect what is right in the sight of all men. ¹⁸If possible, so far as it depends on you, be at peace with all men. ¹⁹Never take your own revenge, beloved, but leave room for the wrath of God, for it is written, "Vengeance is Mine, I will repay," says the Lord. ²⁰"But if your enemy is hungry, feed him, and if he is thirsty, give him a drink; for in so doing you will heap burning coals on his head." ²¹Do not be overcome by evil, but overcome evil with good.

Living Holy Lives (12:1–2)

Paul called for believers in Jesus Christ to present their bodies as living and holy sacrifices to God, our "spiritual service of worship" (Romans 12:1). His statement conjures up the image of incense offered in worship. James 4:14 says, "You are just a vapor that appears for a little while and then vanishes away." We offer up our bodies as incense to God with every breath we breathe and every day we live. By God's grace, we are to live holy and transformed lives that are pleasing to God.

Living the transformed life in Christ begins with repentance. We often think of repentance as a decision to stop doing bad things, kind of a spiritual New Year's resolution. We liken repentance to putting off bad habits or even adding good habits to our daily living. But repentance is much more than that. The Greek word for repentance is *metanoia*. This word is the combination of two words: *meta* meaning *to transform or change*; and *noia*, meaning *mind*. The literal meaning of repentance is *transformation of the mind*. Consequently, to repent is to think differently. Some would call this experiencing *a paradigm shift*. We see things differently. We think differently. We act differently. All the rules change. This is what the Apostle Paul described in Romans 12:2 as being "transformed by the renewing of your mind."

John the Baptist prepared the way for Jesus by preaching that everyone should "repent, for the kingdom of heaven is at hand" (Matthew 3:2). Jesus underscored the importance of repentance when he launched his public ministry with the same message (Matt. 4:17). When Jesus sent out the Twelve in teams of two, "they went out and preached that men should repent" (Mark 6:12). When Jesus' followers considered the suffering caused by human brutality and natural disaster, Jesus used the occasion to warn, "unless you repent, you will all likewise perish" (Luke 18:5).

We don't like to think about repentance primarily because we don't want to change the way we live and think. We prefer to add religion to our schedules and live pretty much like everyone else. We like the fact that Jesus died for our sins and rose from the dead to give us the gift of eternal life, but we don't really want God to meddle with our lives. After all, we think we are pretty good people and have already figured out how things work.

Living as Members of the Body (12:3–8)

Transformation does not occur in isolation. We need one another in order to become the people God wants us to be. Imagine what would have happened to the Apostle Paul if Ananias had not found him in Damascus (Acts 9:10–19) or if Barnabas had not recommended Paul to the leaders in Jerusalem (Acts 9:26–28) and later brought him to Antioch (Acts 11:20–26; 13:1–3).

Paul likens Christian community to the body. We are each unique, given different gifts. Our gifts are only realized as we exercise our gifts

> ## Overcoming Evil with Good
>
> On a crisp October morning in 2006, Charles Roberts entered a single room school nestled in a corn field near Lancaster, Pennsylvania. Thirty minutes later, he had killed five innocent Amish girls. The nation was shocked by the horror of this brutal murder. But the nation was also surprised by the Amish response. The Amish men and women arrived at the murderer's home the next day, embraced his family, and offered comfort and forgiveness. The Amish are known widely for living close-knit agrarian lives. But, on this occasion, they made headlines by practicing Paul's instructions to "overcome evil with good" (Rom. 12:21).[4] How can you respond in a similar situation?

as members of the larger body. Ananias and Barnabas helped Paul discover his unique gifting as Apostle to the Gentiles. In a similar way, other believers help us discover our own gifts, just as we are to help them discover theirs.

The list of gifts Paul includes in this passage is not exhaustive. That is why they differ slightly from the list of gifts in 1 Corinthians 12. The list is representative, just as his reference to the hand, eye, foot, and ear in 1 Corinthians were representative of the physical organs. There are many other members of our physical body, and there are many other gifts of the Spirit. Every member is unique. Every member has something to contribute to the body of Christ as God's instrument for redemption and transformation.

Many times we only see members of the church in terms of what they can do to promote the programs of the church. But God is interested in how the church functions as his body to empower and equip every member to be effective in the world. Instead of asking, *What can you do to help our church?* we need to ask, *What is God's vision for you? How has God uniquely gifted you? How can we help you fulfill God's vision for your life and use your unique gifts for God's glory?*

When considering the gifts of the Spirit, it is always important to differentiate between the gifts of the Spirit and the fruit of the Spirit. The gifts of the Spirit are unique for each believer in order to accomplish God's purposes. The fruit of the Spirit is common to all believers to reflect God's character: "love, joy, peace, patience, kindness, goodness, faithfulness, gentleness, self-control" (Galatians 5:22–23). We each have different gifts. We all should demonstrate the fruit of the Spirit.

Living with Attitude (12:3, 10–13, 15)

Sometimes what we do is not as important as why we do it or how we do it. Our attitude can validate or invalidate our actions. Only God's grace can create the right attitude for living transformed lives. The New Testament gives the impression that before Paul experienced God's grace, he was arrogant, conceited, self-willed, and combative. But God's grace changed him, not all at once, but throughout his life. As a result, the persecutor of women and children authored 1 Corinthians 13, the greatest treatise on love in literature.

The attitude Paul described is one of humility. Our task is not to be critical of our fellow believers but to look to ourselves first (Matt. 7:3–5) and to treat others with love and respect.

Living with Authenticity (12:9–13)

The key to living the transformed life is authenticity. This is what it means to "love . . . without hypocrisy" (Rom. 12:9). To be authentic does not mean we are perfect. It means we are real, that we are honest and without pretense. Something that is authentic is not necessarily perfect. In fact, often that which is truly authentic is seriously flawed. For instance, the original Declaration of Independence, housed in the Rotunda for the Charters of Freedom in Washington, D.C., is fragile and badly faded.[3] Most reproductions are of better quality and much more easily read. But, the reproductions are not authentic.

To be authentic is to be real. This was one of the core values in Jesus' teaching. He seeks out people who are real and authentic, who shun pretense and, above all, refuse to be hypocritical. When you examine the people in the Bible who followed Jesus, you find people who were imperfect. What set them apart as followers of Jesus was their willingness to be authentic. Peter started his journey with Jesus by confessing, "I am a sinful man" (Luke 5:8). Thomas openly shared his doubts and misgivings. James and John were ambitious. Jesus often referred to his disciples as people of "little faith" (Matt. 6:30; 8:26; 14:31; 16:8; Luke 12:28).

To live transformed lives we must cultivate authenticity in our behavior and our relationships. We are to "abhor what is evil" and "cling to what is good" (Rom. 12:9). The word Paul used here for "evil" is *apostugountes*, which occurs only this once in the New Testament. It means *total repulsion*. We are to be repulsed by anything evil. But we are to embrace the good, *kollomenoi*, like lovers driven by passion uniting their lives together in marriage.

Demonstrating the Transformed Life (12:14–21)

In verses 14–21 Paul described the transformed life that results from repentance. His source for this description clearly is related to the Sermon on the Mount (Matt. 5—7). If you want to know Jesus' *flight plan* for flying right-side up, study these verses and the Sermon on the Mount. The emphasis is on obedience more than knowledge. We must

"Amazing Grace"

Perhaps no song in the English language is better known than "Amazing Grace." John Newton wrote the song about 1772. Born in England in 1725, Newton spent his early life in the slave trade, eventually serving as captain of a slave ship. But his conversion to Christ changed everything. He gave up the slave trade and gave himself to the ministry of the gospel.

Newton is credited with influencing William Wilberforce[5] to remain in politics in England in order to abolish the slave trade. This effort succeeded in 1807, just months before Newton's death. Newton asked that the following inscription be included on his headstone: "John Newton, Clerk, once an infidel and libertine, a servant of slaves in Africa, was, by the rich mercy of our Lord and Saviour Jesus Christ, preserved, restored, pardoned, and appointed to preach the faith he had long labored to destroy."[6] God uses repentant hearts and transformed lives to change the world.

have more than knowledge about the Bible; we must put the instructions of Jesus into practice. Jesus concluded his Sermon on the Mount by reminding us that what we do with his instructions is more important than what we know about them (Matt. 7:21, 24–27). When Paul became a believer, he chose to hear the words of Jesus and act on them.

Consider the contrast between Paul as a young man and his instructions in this chapter. The Book of Acts described Paul in his youth as "breathing threats and murder against the disciples of the Lord" (Acts 9:1). Prior to meeting Jesus, Paul was filled with anger and selfish ambition. He believed in the power of force and violence. But when he met Jesus, he repented. He learned to bless his enemies, to do good for those who despised him and abused him, to put the interest of others ahead of his own. He refused to consider revenge and chose to forgive. Paul started his life flying upside down. After meeting Jesus, he began to fly right-side up.

QUESTIONS

1. What has been your experience of repentance? What difference would repentance make in your life today?

LESSON 9: *Live in Faithfulness to God*

2. What gifts has God given you to bless others? What gifts do you see in fellow believers in your church? What gifts do they see in you?

3. When have you seen someone overcome evil with good?

4. What are some ways in which you can apply practically one or more of Paul's teachings in Romans 12?

NOTES

1. See www.cbc.ca/world/story/2000/06/23/kennedyplane000623.html. Accessed 1/22/09.
2. Dallas Willard, *The Divine Conspiracy* (New York: HarperOne, 1998).
3. www.archives.gov/exhibits/charters/declaration.html. Accessed 1/22/09.
4. See http://news.bbc.co.uk/2/hi/americas/6052758.stm. Accessed 1/22/09.
5. The movie "Amazing Grace," telling the story of William Wiberforce and the abolition of slavery in England, was released in 2006. To watch a video about the song, Amazing Grace, go to: http://www.amazinggracemovie.com/storyofamazinggrace.php. Accessed 1/29/09.
6. http://www.johnnewtoncenter.org/johnnewton.htm. Accessed 1/29/09.

LESSON TEN
Engage in God's Mission Together

FOCAL TEXTS
Acts 4:32–35;
2 Corinthians 8:1–9;
1 Corinthians 12:4–13;
1 Peter 2:6–10

BACKGROUND
Acts 4:32–35;
1 Corinthians 12;
2 Corinthians 8—9;
1 Peter 2:6–10

MAIN IDEA
God's people are to use their diverse gifts in engaging in God's mission together.

QUESTION TO EXPLORE
Do you need to increase your commitment to serving God with your fellow church members rather than alone if at all?

STUDY AIM
To decide on at least one way in which I will use my gifts to serve God with fellow believers

QUICK READ
Authentic disciples are called into relationship with one another.

To get to Cottonwood Baptist Church near Dublin, Texas, you turn south at the traffic light in Dublin. Then you drive five miles and turn into the gravel parking lot. If it's Sunday, you'll see many pickup trucks among the vehicles parked there. The church building is located behind a grove of live oak trees, and the air is usually heavy with the smell of cattle.

The pastor at Cottonwood is Mike Fritcher. Mike came to the church as a seminary student about twenty-five years ago. He thought he would be at the twenty-three-member church about eighteen months. Instead, God told him to stay. He took a job as a substitute teacher to make a living and began leading the people to love God and love one another. In 2001 he was persuaded to take a trip to China. Afterward, he invited Mike Stroope, missions professor at Truett Theological Seminary, to lead the church in a weekend missions focus. Dr. Stroope challenged them to cast their vision to the ends of the earth and God would fill in everything in between. They did.

Cottonwood Baptist Church has sent five families to China and others to Africa. They are working among the Tarahumara, an unreached people group in Mexico, and praying about going to Indonesia. Today more than 900 people drive from the open country around Dublin to worship at Cottonwood.

Somewhere along the way, Cottonwood Baptist started referring to themselves as *the body*. Everything they do, they do as a *body* of believers and as members of *the body* of Christ. The language and the story of Cottonwood Baptist sound a lot like the language and the story of the New Testament.

ACTS 4:32–35

³² And the congregation of those who believed were of one heart and soul; and not one of them claimed that anything belonging to him was his own, but all things were common property to them. ³³ And with great power the apostles were giving testimony to the resurrection of the Lord Jesus, and abundant grace was upon them all. ³⁴ For there was not a needy person among them, for all who were owners of land or houses would sell them and bring the proceeds of the sales ³⁵ and lay them at the apostles' feet, and they would be distributed to each as any had need.

LESSON 10: *Engage in God's Mission Together*

2 CORINTHIANS 8:1–9

¹Now, brethren, we wish to make known to you the grace of God which has been given in the churches of Macedonia, ²that in a great ordeal of affliction their abundance of joy and their deep poverty overflowed in the wealth of their liberality. ³For I testify that according to their ability, and beyond their ability, they gave of their own accord, ⁴begging us with much urging for the favor of participation in the support of the saints, ⁵and this, not as we had expected, but they first gave themselves to the Lord and to us by the will of God. ⁶So we urged Titus that as he had previously made a beginning, so he would also complete in you this gracious work as well. ⁷But just as you abound in everything, in faith and utterance and knowledge and in all earnestness and in the love we inspired in you, see that you abound in this gracious work also. ⁸I am not speaking this as a command, but as proving through the earnestness of others the sincerity of your love also. ⁹For you know the grace of our Lord Jesus Christ, that though He was rich, yet for your sake He became poor, so that you through His poverty might become rich.

1 CORINTHIANS 12:4–13

⁴Now there are varieties of gifts, but the same Spirit. ⁵And there are varieties of ministries, and the same Lord. ⁶There are varieties of effects, but the same God who works all things in all persons. ⁷But to each one is given the manifestation of the Spirit for the common good. ⁸For to one is given the word of wisdom through the Spirit, and to another the word of knowledge according to the same Spirit; ⁹to another faith by the same Spirit, and to another gifts of healing by the one Spirit, ¹⁰and to another the effecting of miracles, and to another prophecy, and to another the distinguishing of spirits, to another various kinds of tongues, and to another the interpretation of tongues. ¹¹But one and the same Spirit works all these things, distributing to each one individually just as He wills. ¹²For even as the body is one and yet has many members, and all the members of the body, though they are many,

are one body, so also is Christ. ¹³For by one Spirit we were all baptized into one body, whether Jews or Greeks, whether slaves or free, and we were all made to drink of one Spirit.

1 PETER 2:6–10

⁶For this is contained in Scripture: "Behold, I lay in Zion a choice stone, a precious corner stone, And he who believes in Him will not be disappointed." ⁷This precious value, then, is for you who believe; but for those who disbelieve, "The stone which the builders rejected, This became the very corner stone," ⁸and, "A stone of stumbling and a rock of offense"; for they stumble because they are disobedient to the word, and to this doom they were also appointed. ⁹But you are a chosen race, a royal priesthood, a holy nation, a people for God's own possession, so that you may proclaim the excellencies of Him who has called you out of darkness into His marvelous light; ¹⁰for you once were not a people, but now you are the people of God; you had not received mercy, but now you have received mercy.

Holding All Things in Common (Acts 4:32–35)

This passage describes the church in Jerusalem following Pentecost, the occasion when God sent the Holy Spirit as Jesus promised (John 16:7–15; Acts 1:8, 2:16–18). The picture of the church immediately following Pentecost is a unique snapshot of the body of Christ in infant beauty.

The practice of holding all things in common as described in Acts 4:32–35 would not continue for long. The story of Ananias and Sapphira that immediately follows (Acts 5) and the complaint among the Hellenestic widows (Acts 6) reflect the problems that soon arose. But this passage gives us a remarkable image of what the body of Christ could look like when all our human shortcomings disappear and the fullness of the Holy Spirit is come.

When the body of Christ is filled with the Holy Spirit, we are generous. What we have is not our own. Generosity cannot be coerced. It must be of the heart. When we are healthy as the body of Christ, we are spontaneously generous to one another.

When the body of Christ is filled with the Holy Spirit, we are one in heart and soul. We Baptists are famous for our arguments and disagreements, but when we are healthy as the body of Christ we experience unity of heart and soul. This was Jesus' great concern and the object of his longest prayer (John 17), "that they may all be one; even as you, Father, are in Me and I in You, that they also may be in Us, so that the world may believe that You sent Me" (John 17:21).

When the body of Christ is filled with the Holy Spirit, we give powerful witness to the resurrection of Jesus. We live in a culture that is increasingly composed of many and varied religious groups, including Islam, Buddhism, Hinduism, Judaism, and New Age. We live in a secular self-help culture where ten-step formulas to recovery and success abound. The body of Christ must focus on the message that makes it unique: that God raised Jesus Christ from the dead. This is no mere philosophy competing against other philosophies or religions. This is an historic event that transforms everything we know about God, the world, and ourselves. One of the elements I like best about

GEORGE W. TRUETT

George W. Truett (1867–1944) was perhaps the greatest Baptist leader and statesman of the twentieth century.[1] As a young adult, he saved financially-strapped Baylor University, even before enrolling as a freshman. He served First Baptist Church, Dallas, Texas, as pastor for forty-seven years and led it to become one of the most influential churches in the world. Among many other accomplishments, he served as a leader of the Baptist World Alliance. But George W. Truett did not choose the ministry. He planned to study law. When he was twenty-three, the Baptist church at Whitewright, Texas, called a business meeting and voted unanimously to ordain him to the ministry against his protests. Truett later said of the event, "There I was, against a whole church, against a church profoundly moved. There was not a dry eye in the house—one of the supremely solemn hours in a church's life. I was thrown into the stream, and just had to swim."[2] Sometimes the body of Christ recognizes gifts in us we cannot see.

> ## Your Spiritual Gifts
>
> - Ask members of your class or group to describe what they see as your spiritual gifts.
> - Make a list of ways you are currently using your spiritual gifts to fulfill God's purposes.
> - Make a list of possible ways to use your spiritual gifts more effectively for God's purposes.
> - Examine your budget and your giving patterns. Are you demonstrating generosity as a steward of your resources? How could you adjust your budget to become more generous in your giving? Plan incremental increases in your giving over the next five years.

most African-American churches is that they seldom conduct a service in which they do not proclaim the resurrection with power. Sooner or later the message focuses on the fact that Jesus rose up from the grave!

When the body of Christ is filled with the Holy Spirit, we sense God's grace and radiate it in our lives. I have sometimes felt God's grace just walking into a church. Too, I have sometimes sensed the painful absence of God's grace in a congregation. Recently as I flew from Dallas to Denver, a young Hispanic man sat next to me. He asked me what I was reading. I told him it was a spiritual book about the soul. That exchange opened an hour-long conversation about God's glory, our sin, and God's redemption and grace in Jesus. I found he was a new believer with a young wife and children. As we landed he said, "When you sat down I sensed a spirit of peace about you. That is why I asked you what you were reading." May we always radiate God's grace as members of Christ's body.

Giving Beyond Our Means (2 Corinthians 8:1–9)

This passage is addressed to the believers in Corinth, a prosperous Greek city where Paul spent eighteen months starting a church (Acts 18:1–18).

LESSON 10: *Engage in God's Mission Together* 115

Some of the churches Paul referred to in the province of Macedonia (such as Philippi, Thessalonica, Berea) were started on his second missionary journey, as was Corinth, in the province of Achaia (Acts 16:1—18:23). Ancient Macedonia is now divided among modern Albania, Macedonia, Bulgaria, and northern Greece. Unlike prosperous Corinth, the region of Macedonia was suffering a serious economic recession at the time of the writing of 2 Corinthians. Paul and his companions were urging the churches they had started to contribute to an offering for the believers in Jerusalem, who were suffering serious economic stress partly due to the economy but largely due to persecution.

Paul used the example of the believers in Macedonia to inspire the prosperous Corinthians to give more generously. In spite of their poverty, the Christians in Macedonia had begged for the opportunity to give.

When I served as executive director for the Minnesota-Wisconsin Baptist Convention, one of my greatest pleasures was to work with the Hmong Baptists. The Hmong, a native people from the mountain regions of Laos and our staunchest allies during the Vietnam War, came to the United States as refugees. They had suffered enormous persecution following the fall of Vietnam. Most of them relocated to Minnesota-Wisconsin. Many turned from their native animism and embraced Jesus Christ as Lord. When the Red River of the North flooded Grand Forks, South Dakota, cresting above fifty feet, the Hmong were among the first to respond for disaster relief. Typically short in stature, they stood on boxes to stir huge pots of food to feed those evacuated from the flood. With low-income jobs, they were among the first to raise an offering. The Hmong women soon became the largest single group at Woman's Missionary Union meetings, urging their churches to support mission efforts. Like the Macedonians, they led the way in giving out of their ordeal of affliction and abundance of joy.

Have you had exposure to real poverty? When I slogged through mud in the slums of Brazil, stepped across open running sewage, and saw families crouching under makeshift shelters of styrofoam and plastic, I returned to my room and wept. How much does God require of us to bear one another's burdens in a world of such vast poverty?

Golden West Christian Church is made up of Cambodian believers in Los Angeles, California. It is a small church. Most of the members have low-income jobs. The pastor is a survivor of the Killing Fields in

Cambodia. He has led the entire church to embrace missions to their homeland. Many of the members give one-third of their income to start churches in Cambodia. One widow begged the church to accept a gift of all her savings following her daughter's death in order to build a church in Cambodia. This one small church has started more than 300 churches in Northwest Cambodia and seen 20,000 people come to faith in Christ. Like the Corinthian believers, we need to be inspired by our brothers and sisters who "give beyond their means" so that we might give sacrificially for the gospel.

Gifted for a Purpose (1 Corinthians 12:4–13)

God has made each of us unique. We know this is true with our DNA. It is also true in many other ways, including the ways God has gifted us. Most of us spend our lives trying to be like someone else or to live up to the expectations of others. We spend enormous energy, and we often feel we have failed when we try to live from the *outside in*. God wants us to live from the *inside out*. What is unique and special about you? How has God gifted you for his purposes in the world?

You might look at the gifts that Paul lists here and say, *None of those fit me*. That is okay. Paul did not give this list of gifts to exhaust the list of possibilities. Rather they are representative of the many gifts God gives to believers. Just as our physical bodies are intricate, complex, and mysterious, so are the gifts of the Spirit.

The real point is that we should help one another discover our unique gifts, and then we should use those gifts to benefit the larger purposes of God. Instead of trying to make other people look or act like us, and instead of trying to look like and act like other people, we need to free one another up to be special and unique in the way God has made us. When all of us are using God's unique gifts to fulfill God's vision for our lives, incredible things happen.

Royal Priesthood (1 Peter 2:6–10)

Several years ago I started teaching a class entitled "The Catholic Connection." The church offered the class for those who grew up with a

Catholic background but were searching and asking questions. We provided a safe place where they could ask their questions and explore what the Bible said. One of the questions most of them asked was, *Why don't Baptists have priests?*

To find the answer we turned to this passage in 1 Peter. Participants in the class were often surprised to learn that every believer is a priest. We all have direct access to God through Jesus Christ. Jesus Christ is the cornerstone. How we respond to Jesus makes all the difference. Since we have believed in Jesus, he has made us a royal priesthood to share with others the glory of God who called us out of darkness. Our testimony is not about ourselves but about God and God's goodness.

Even Baptists divide believers between clergy and laity, the professionals and the amateurs. But there are no amateur believers. In fact, in the first century, there was no clergy. We are all part of one body, each uniquely gifted and equipped to build up one another for God's purposes, that God's kingdom will come on earth as it is in heaven.

Conclusion

The church functions properly as the body of Christ when it embraces its purpose. The church was not established to make us feel better. It was not created to make us successful. Rather the church was created as the body of Christ in the world for the same purpose for which Christ came: to seek and save the lost. When a body of believers comes together on mission, they discover the unique gifting of God to fulfill God's purposes to the ends of the earth.

QUESTIONS

1. What was your most generous gift to missions last year? Why did you give your gift? How did you feel when you gave it?

2. What spiritual gifts has God given you? What spiritual gifts do other believers see in you?

3. What has been your most spirit-filled church experience?

4. When 1 Peter 2:9 says you are a "royal priesthood," what privileges and responsibilities does this imply?

NOTES

1. See www.sbhla.org/biogtruett.htm and www.tshaonline.org/handbook/online/articles/TT/ftr16.html Accessed 1/23/09.
2. Clyde E. Fant, Jr., and William M. Pinson, Jr., *20 Centuries of Great Preaching* (Word Books, Publisher: Waco, Texas, 1971), VIII: 133–134, citing Powhatan W. James, *George W. Truett: A Biography* (New York: Macmillan Co., 1945), 48–49.

LESSON ELEVEN
Tell the Good News of Redemption and Reconciliation

FOCAL TEXTS
2 Corinthians 5:11–21;
Colossians 1:24–29

BACKGROUND
2 Corinthians 4—5;
Colossians 1:24–29

MAIN IDEA
Participating in God's mission means telling the good news of redemption and reconciliation.

QUESTION TO EXPLORE
Do your actions and the actions of your church demonstrate that telling the good news of redemption and reconciliation is important?

STUDY AIM
To analyze how well I am extending God's offer of redemption and reconciliation and to decide on at least one step I will take to share the gospel

QUICK READ
God has entrusted to every believer the ministry of redemption and reconciliation.

The movie *Chariots of Fire* tells the true story of Eric Liddell, a gifted athlete from Scotland who refused to compete on Sunday in the 1924 Olympics because of his Christian beliefs. As a result he forfeited his place in the 100-meter dash, his strongest event. Instead he competed in the 400-meter race on Monday. He not only won the Olympic gold medal, but he also broke the record for the 400.[1]

One of the most moving scenes occurs in the meadows of Scotland. Eric's cousin, Jenny, is trying to persuade him to give up competing in the Olympics and to follow his calling as a missionary to China. He turns to his cousin and says, "Jenny, God made me, and he made me fast. And when I run, I feel his pleasure!" After winning the Olympics, Eric Liddell followed Christ's call to China, where he died in a Japanese prison camp in 1945.

The compulsion to serve God that Liddell felt must have been similar to how Paul felt regarding his compulsion to share the good news of Jesus Christ. Paul said, "For this purpose also I labor, striving according to His power, which mightily works within me" (Colossians 1:29).

2 CORINTHIANS 5:11–21

[11]Therefore, knowing the fear of the Lord, we persuade men, but we are made manifest to God; and I hope that we are made manifest also in your consciences. [12]We are not again commending ourselves to you but are giving you an occasion to be proud of us, so that you will have an answer for those who take pride in appearance and not in heart. [13]For if we are beside ourselves, it is for God; if we are of sound mind, it is for you. [14]For the love of Christ controls us, having concluded this, that one died for all, therefore all died; [15]and He died for all, so that they who live might no longer live for themselves, but for Him who died and rose again on their behalf. [16]Therefore from now on we recognize no one according to the flesh; even though we have known Christ according to the flesh, yet now we know Him in this way no longer. [17]Therefore if anyone is in Christ, he is a new creature; the old things passed away; behold, new things have come. [18]Now all these things are from God, who reconciled us to Himself through Christ and gave us the ministry of reconciliation, [19]namely, that

God was in Christ reconciling the world to Himself, not counting their trespasses against them, and He has committed to us the word of reconciliation. [20]Therefore, we are ambassadors for Christ, as though God were making an appeal through us; we beg you on behalf of Christ, be reconciled to God. [21]He made Him who knew no sin to be sin on our behalf, so that we might become the righteousness of God in Him.

COLOSSIANS 1:24–29

[24]Now I rejoice in my sufferings for your sake, and in my flesh I do my share on behalf of His body, which is the church, in filling up what is lacking in Christ's afflictions. [25]Of this church I was made a minister according to the stewardship from God bestowed on me for your benefit, so that I might fully carry out the preaching of the word of God, [26]that is, the mystery which has been hidden from the past ages and generations, but has now been manifested to His saints, [27]to whom God willed to make known what is the riches of the glory of this mystery among the Gentiles, which is Christ in you, the hope of glory. [28]We proclaim Him, admonishing every man and teaching every man with all wisdom, so that we may present every man complete in Christ. [29]For this purpose also I labor, striving according to His power, which mightily works within me.

The Motive (2 Corinthians 5:11–14)

Paul indicated two motives that compelled him to bear witness to Jesus Christ. The first was his awe of God. This is what he referred to when he wrote, "Therefore knowing the fear of the Lord. . . " (2 Corinthians 5:11). He used the world *phobos*, from which we derive our English word *phobia*. But we would be wrong to conclude that Paul witnessed because he felt coerced to do so. Instead, he bore witness to Christ because he was overwhelmed with awe of the majesty and greatness of God who sent his Son to reconcile the world.

The second motive Paul referred to is the love of Christ. He wrote, "For the love of Christ controls us. . . ." (2 Cor. 5:14). This love is two-directional. First, Christ loved us. He died for us while we were still sinners and enemies with God (Romans 5:8). Christ initiated the love relationship by his sacrifice (1 John 4:10). Second, we love Christ. Having been loved by Christ to such an extent, how can we help but love him? Those who have experienced Christ's love "live . . . no longer for themselves, but for Him who died and rose again on their behalf" (2 Cor. 5:15).

Everyone who encounters an awe-inspiring experience feels compelled to talk about it. Those who stand on the rim of the Grand Canyon often come away awed by its expanse, beauty, and grandeur. They feel compelled to show their photographs, even though they know that words and pictures fall far short of the reality.

When a young couple fall in love, they not only want to be with each other as much as possible, but they feel compelled to tell others about the person who has claimed their heart. Those whom we love the most occupy our minds, invade our dreams, and enter into our conversation with others.

Over the years I have had the opportunity to observe many missionaries who have gone to the ends of the earth to bear witness for Christ. Without exception, those who were effective were motivated by the awe and love of God. They witnessed out of a worship and love relationship with Jesus. Other motives ultimately leave us frustrated, jaded, cynical, and compromised.

If you and your church would be effective witnesses for Christ, focus on God. Worship God in awe and adoration. Cultivate a personal loving relationship with God that captivates your heart. There are many methods to share the good news of Jesus Christ, but nothing can replace a heart that is *beside itself* (2 Cor. 5:13) with joy about God. Start here: stand in awe of God; fall in love with Jesus.

The Ministry (2 Corinthians 5:15–21)

From the moment sin entered the world, God has been at work to redeem and reconcile, not only people, but all of creation. The thrust of the Bible is to tell the story of God's redeeming and reconciling work. Now God has invited us to enter into his work.

> ## CENTERED ON JESUS
>
> The first-century believers developed a consistent message that they preached wherever they went. It was referred to as the *kerygma*, a Greek term meaning *proclamation* or *announcement* (see 1 Cor. 1:21; 2 Timothy 4:17; Titus 1:3). For the *kerygma* itself, see Acts 3:13–19; 10:37–43. If you examine these passages that summarize the *kerygma*, you will see that the focus is on Jesus. First-century believers did not talk about their churches, their preachers, their programs, or themselves. They talked about Jesus.

God has given us "the ministry of reconciliation" and made us "ambassadors for Christ" (5:18, 20). The word Paul used for "ministry" is from the Greek word *diakonos* (2 Cor. 5:18). This word is most often translated *servant* (Matthew 20:26–28; John 12:26). The word Paul used for "ambassador" translates the Greek word *presbeuo* (2 Cor. 5:20). An "ambassador" represents someone else. Ambassadors do not represent themselves. Rather, someone in authority has delegated authority to the ambassador to represent him. As ministers of reconciliation and ambassadors for Christ, we are stewards of this amazing work of God to redeem and reconcile the world to himself (Colossians 1:25).

Stewards of the story. As ministers of reconciliation and ambassadors for Christ, we are stewards of the story of Jesus—why Jesus came, what Jesus did, who Jesus is. To be ministers of reconciliation and ambassadors for Christ, we must tell the story of how God sent Jesus, how he died for our sins, and how he rose from the dead.

In study I have done of how to train people in personal evangelism, I have discovered that we can easily engage people in conversation about the church and its programs. Too, some people are interested in arguing about religion and theology. But when we turn the conversation to Jesus, everything changes. Even the Muslim world holds Jesus in high esteem as a prophet. Mahatma Gandhi patterned his life after the life and teachings of Jesus. Even those who reject the church and organized religion are attracted to Jesus. So, if we would be ministers of reconciliation and ambassadors for God, we must talk about Jesus.

> ## The Nations and You
>
> A couple of years ago our daughter went on a mission trip to Andhra Pradesh, a state in India. At the same time, my wife and I visited Lubbock, Texas. When we checked into the hotel, I asked the clerk where he was from. He said he was from India. I told him our daughter was visiting Andhra Pradesh. He said, "I'm from Andhra Pradesh." I visited with him about Jesus and gave him a copy of my book, *The Jesus Encounter*.[2] Later he wrote and said he had read my book and shared it with his Hindu friends and that they were talking about it. My daughter went to India to witness to someone in Andhra Pradesh. I went to Lubbock! Whom is God bringing from other nations to your community?

Stewards of our story. Paul referred to the unique effect of the gospel in every believer when he said, "If anyone is in Christ, he is a new creature; the old things passed away; behold, new things have com" (2 Cor. 5:17). God has given each believer a personal story to tell about how God has transformed his or her life. People will argue about church and religion, but they cannot argue about your personal experience. You alone are the authority about how God has changed you through your faith in Jesus Christ. You can share with family, friends, and people you meet how God has made you a new creation. What was your life like before you became a believer? How did you come to faith in Jesus? What difference has God made in your life since? The answers to these questions are usually very clear to those who come to faith as adults. For those who trusted Jesus at a young age, the difference is sometimes most clearly evident in what their lives would have been like without Jesus. God has gifted you with a special and unique story that makes you a minister of redemption and an ambassador for Christ.

The Mystery (Colossians 1:24–29)

God's work of reconciliation and redemption is a mystery. We can never fathom fully what God is doing and how God is working. God has said,

"As the heavens are higher than the earth, So are My ways higher than your ways and My thoughts than your thoughts" (Isaiah 55:9).

Paul lived in awe and humility as he marveled at the "mystery" of God (Col. 1:26). In this life we always "see in a mirror dimly" and can only "know in part" (1 Corinthians 13:12). We must never become so familiar with church and religion that we lose a sense of the mystery of God.

The "mystery" of Christ in you. The mystery to which Paul referred in Colossians 1:26–27 is the great mystery that was hidden for ages. We find clues to this mystery in the prophets (Jeremiah 31:31–34; Ezekiel 11:19; 36:26–27). We see this mystery unfolding at Pentecost (Acts 2) when the Holy Spirit was given just as Jesus promised (John 16:7–14). Jesus promises to come into our hearts if we invite him (Revelation 3:20). When Paul tried to live life in his own power, he failed (Romans 7:14–24). Only the mystery of Christ within Paul could enable him to live the Christ-filled life (Rom. 7:25—8:2; Gal. 2:20). It is God "who is at work in you, both to will and to work for His good pleasure" (Philippians 2:13).

The principle of "Christ in you" (Col. 1:27) cannot be dissected or explained in scientific or psychological terms. At this point our faith takes us into a "mystery" that defies modern definitions. But, for those who know Jesus Christ by faith, this reality shapes their world more profoundly than any other experience. We cannot be ministers of reconciliation and redemption in our own power. Redemption and reconciliation are the work of God and require God's presence within us. When we repent of our sins and invite Jesus Christ into our lives, we become new creations. We become ministers of reconciliation and redemption.

The "mystery" of the nations. Paul referred to a second mystery in this work of redemption and reconciliation: the mystery of the nations. He enlarged on this "mystery" in Ephesians 3:4–6. The Greek word translated "Gentiles" is *ethne,* the root word for our term *ethnic.* This is the same word Jesus used when he gave the command in the Great Commission to "make disciples of all the nations" (Matt. 28:19–20). The word can refer to races, cultures, tribes, and people-groups.

This is a very important concept in God's plan for redemption and reconciliation. God started his redemption plan by calling Abraham and promised to bless him so that he would become a "blessing to the nations" (Genesis 12:1–2; 18:18; 22:15–18). Isaiah, looking forward to the Messiah, recognized that God's redemption included all the *ethne,* the "nations" (Isaiah 42:6; 49:6; 60:3). When Jesus was born, God led the Magi from the East (probably modern Iraq and Iran) to include the nations. When Joseph and Mary brought the baby Jesus to Jerusalem, the prophet Simeon declared, "For my eyes have seen Your salvation, Which You have prepared in the presence of all peoples, A Light of revelation to the Gentiles [*ethne*], And the glory of Your people Israel" (Luke 2:30–32). In Revelation John described the ultimate result of God's redemptive work in Heaven: "After these things I looked, and behold, a great multitude which no one could count, from every nation and all tribes and peoples and tongues, standing before the throne and before the Lamb, clothed in white robes, and palm branches were in their hands; and they cry out with a loud voice, saying, 'Salvation to our God who sits on the throne, and to the Lamb'" (Rev. 7:9–10).

Conclusion

We are witnessing the greatest movement of people groups in the history of the world. Many are moving to the United States. More than 100 languages are spoken in Houston, Texas. This movement of people with different ethnicities, languages, and cultures creates new opportunities for redemption and reconciliation. What is happening in your community? How are you and your church engaged as stewards and ambassadors of the gospel?

QUESTIONS

1. When was the last time you talked with someone about Jesus?

2. What different ethnic groups live in your community?

3. Have you ever been on a mission trip outside the United States? If so, how did it affect you?

4. How does your church equip believers to share their faith with others?

NOTES

1. Eric Liddell. (2009). In *Encyclopædia Britannica*. Accessed 1/29/09, from Encyclopædia Britannica Online: http://www.britannica.com/EBchecked/topic/339751/Eric-Liddell.
2. *The Jesus Encounter* is available at www.authenticdisciple.com.

LESSON TWELVE
Minister to People's Physical Needs

FOCAL TEXTS
Deuteronomy 10:14–19; Amos 5:21–24; Matthew 25:31–46

BACKGROUND
Deuteronomy 10:14–19; Amos 5:18–24; Matthew 25:31–46; Luke 10:25–37; 16:19–31

MAIN IDEA
Participating in God's mission means ministering to people's physical needs.

QUESTION TO EXPLORE
Do your actions and the actions of your church demonstrate that ministering to people's physical needs is important?

STUDY AIM
To analyze how well I follow biblical teachings about ministering to people's physical needs and to decide on at least one step I will take to do so

QUICK READ
While churches tend to worry about worship styles, buildings, budgets, and church attendance, God is concerned about what happens to people in need, including the poor, the oppressed, the vulnerable, and the weak of our world.

We live in a world that is wracked with pain. War, corruption, crime, and human need cut a vast swath of suffering across the globe and invade our most remote communities. The faces of victims are flashed on our television screens with disturbing regularity. But God has a different plan, and God calls us to participate in it.

DEUTERONOMY 10:14–19

14 "Behold, to the Lord your God belong heaven and the highest heavens, the earth and all that is in it. 15 "Yet on your fathers did the Lord set His affection to love them, and He chose their descendants after them, even you above all peoples, as it is this day. 16 "So circumcise your heart, and stiffen your neck no longer. 17 "For the Lord your God is the God of gods and the Lord of lords, the great, the mighty, and the awesome God who does not show partiality nor take a bribe. 18 "He executes justice for the orphan and the widow, and shows His love for the alien by giving him food and clothing. 19 "So show your love for the alien, for you were aliens in the land of Egypt.

AMOS 5:21–24

21 "I hate, I reject your festivals, Nor do I delight in your solemn assemblies. 22 "Even though you offer up to Me burnt offerings and your grain offerings, I will not accept them; And I will not even look at the peace offerings of your fatlings. 23 "Take away from Me the noise of your songs; I will not even listen to the sound of your harps. 24 "But let justice roll down like waters And righteousness like an ever-flowing stream.

MATTHEW 25:31–46

31 "But when the Son of Man comes in His glory, and all the angels with Him, then He will sit on His glorious throne. 32 "All the nations will be gathered before Him; and He will separate them from one another, as the shepherd separates the sheep from the

LESSON 12: *Minister to People's Physical Needs* 131

goats; ³³and He will put the sheep on His right, and the goats on the left. ³⁴"Then the King will say to those on His right, 'Come, you who are blessed of My Father, inherit the kingdom prepared for you from the foundation of the world. ³⁵'For I was hungry, and you gave Me something to eat; I was thirsty, and you gave Me something to drink; I was a stranger, and you invited Me in; ³⁶naked, and you clothed Me; I was sick, and you visited Me; I was in prison, and you came to Me.' ³⁷"Then the righteous will answer Him, 'Lord, when did we see You hungry, and feed You, or thirsty, and give You something to drink? ³⁸'And when did we see You a stranger, and invite You in, or naked, and clothe You? ³⁹'When did we see You sick, or in prison, and come to You?' ⁴⁰"The King will answer and say to them, 'Truly I say to you, to the extent that you did it to one of these brothers of Mine, even the least of them, you did it to Me.' ⁴¹"Then He will also say to those on His left, 'Depart from Me, accursed ones, into the eternal fire which has been prepared for the devil and his angels; ⁴²for I was hungry, and you gave Me nothing to eat; I was thirsty, and you gave Me nothing to drink; ⁴³I was a stranger, and you did not invite Me in; naked, and you did not clothe Me; sick, and in prison, and you did not visit Me.' ⁴⁴"Then they themselves also will answer, 'Lord, when did we see You hungry, or thirsty, or a stranger, or naked, or sick, or in prison, and did not take care of You?' ⁴⁵"Then He will answer them, 'Truly I say to you, to the extent that you did not do it to one of the least of these, you did not do it to Me.' ⁴⁶"These will go away into eternal punishment, but the righteous into eternal life."

Love Finds the Weak and the Vulnerable (Deuteronomy 10:14–19)

The Book of Deuteronomy is named for the event described in this chapter, the second giving of the law. *Deutero* means *second* and *nomos* means *law*. This is the second time God gave Moses the Ten Commandments. The first time God gave them to Moses, Moses returned from the mountain to find the Israelites engaged in pagan worship of a golden calf that they fashioned during his absence. He was so enraged that he dashed the stone tablets on the rocks, shattering the tablets (Exodus 32). God in his mercy gave the commandments a second time to Moses (Exod. 34; Deut.10). This time, Moses constructed a box of acacia wood in which to place them. This box came to be known as the ark of the covenant (made popular in modern culture by the Indiana Jones movie, *Raiders of the Lost Ark*). Later the ark contained the stone tablets, Aaron's rod that budded, and a golden jar containing the manna that God gave the Israelites to eat in the wilderness (Hebrews 9:4).

Our focal passage in Deuteronomy makes it abundantly clear that everything God has done was motivated by love. Love is the essence of God's nature and character. Because God loved us, God created and chose the Israelite people through Abraham. Because God loved us, God gave us the Ten Commandments "for your good" (Deut. 10:13). Ultimately, this same love would result in the birth of Jesus, Jesus' death on the cross, and Jesus' resurrection (John 3:16).

The Bible's statement that God chose the Israelites "above all peoples" (Deut. 10:15) does not imply that God chose them for special privileges. God chose them to demonstrate his power and his love by creating a people who previously did not exist (Genesis 12:1–3; 22:15–18). He chose the Israelites in order to bless the world with redemption.

The nature and character of God and God's activity in human history always require a response from the human heart. This is why Moses challenged the people to "circumcise your heart" (Deut. 10:16). Circumcision involves cutting away the outer flesh. In this case, Moses instructed the people to cut away the calloused flesh of their hearts so that they would be tender toward God and one another. Jeremiah made the same appeal centuries later (Jeremiah 4:4). We tend to become self-centered and selfish, callous, and insensitive to those who are not like us. We take care of ourselves, our family and close friends, and those who look like us and belong to our *tribe*. Only God can circumcise our hearts so that we truly love God and care about others (Deut. 30:6).

I recently heard a fellow Baptist share his testimony. He said he had no use for Muslims, especially following the events of 9-11. But he went on a couple of mission trips with his church to work among an unreached Muslim people group. He said soon he no longer saw them as *Muslims*. He saw them as people whom God loved and for whom Christ died. God had *circumcised his heart*.

> ## Buckner International
>
> Buckner International is a vast organization founded in 1879 in Texas by R.C. Buckner with the purpose of caring for widows and orphans based on the New Testament mandate of Jesus Christ. It is now one of the largest private social care agencies in the United States, with ministries all over the world. Buckner works both as a consultant and practitioner to improve the lives of orphans, at-risk children, families, and senior adults around the globe.[1] To find out about volunteering with Buckner, visit www.helporphans.org.

Moses also challenged the people to "stiffen your neck no longer" (10:16). This expression suggests the image of a horse that refuses to respond to the touch of the reins on its neck. It does not obey its master. It insists on its own will, and, in effect, becomes worse than useless. Jesus used a similar image regarding Saul of Tarsus when he confronted him on the road to Damascus and said, "It is hard for you to kick against the goads" (Acts 26:14). We can be very religious and at the same time insist on living our life our own way, pursuing our own career goals, resisting the will of God.

So, what is God's will for us? This passage makes God's will very clear. He wants us to be like him. As Jesus said, "You are to be perfect as your heavenly Father is perfect" (Matt. 5:48). We are to so love God that God's character and God's nature become our own.

God loves the weak and the vulnerable. This characteristic of God is evident throughout Scripture. He does not honor the proud and the powerful. He exalts the weak and the vulnerable, whether it is an old man named Abraham long past the age of fathering a child, Joseph sold into slavery by his brothers, Moses abandoned in the bulrushes, David facing Goliath with a sling, or Jesus born in a manger. Mary captured the character of God in her song when she discovered she would give birth to the Son of God (Luke 1:46–55; see lesson 3). Deuteronomy 10:18 identifies the most vulnerable as orphans, widows, and aliens.

The condition of orphans worldwide is staggering. By one estimate there are more than 140 million orphans worldwide. Many live and work on the streets and are vulnerable to sexual abuse and exploitation.

> ## ISAAC
>
> ISAAC—the Immigration Service and Aid Center—was created by the Baptist General Convention of Texas and Buckner Children and Family Services to help churches respond to the growing need among immigrants in the United States. ISAAC is a nationwide effort to establish a network of local church-based immigration ministries. ISAAC will help local churches and other like-minded organizations set up a federally "recognized" immigration ministry center, which will then be allowed to legally provide immigration assistance. ISAAC also empowers churches to set up ESL/Citizenship Classes and other ministries. To find out more about ISAAC, visit www.isaacproject.org

God also loves the "alien" (Deut. 10:18–19). The Israelites moved to Egypt as refugees during a great famine and later became slave laborers under the oppressive rule of the pharaohs. God reminded them of this fact and exhorted them to love the alien among them.

Love Establishes Justice (Amos 5:21–24)

Amos lived and prophesied in Judah during the eighth century B.C. He was a contemporary of Isaiah, and both lived during the reign of King Uzziah, who ruled the Southern kingdom of Judah.

Toward the end of Uzziah's reign, there was an increasing gap between worship and daily practice. The people thought their lavish worship could appease God while their daily lives were unjust and unethical. Uzziah's reign, characterized overall by faithfulness and prosperity, became increasingly corrupt.

During the last two decades many churches have struggled with what has come to be known as *worship wars*. Churches have divided over styles of music and worship. Church staff members have been fired. Debates have raged over whether to sing traditional hymns with hymnals, organ music, and pianos, or contemporary songs with guitars and drums. God, of course, is not more pleased with one style of music over another. He is pleased by the heart of the worshiper. God seeks people to worship him who practice righteousness and justice during the week, regardless of music and worship styles.

Corruption remains one of the greatest obstacles to health, prosperity, and happiness in the nations of the earth. Where justice and righteousness reign, there people prosper and God is honored. For this purpose God sent Jesus into the world, that we would be transformed into people of righteousness and that justice would reign on the earth (Isaiah 9:2–7).

Love in Practice (Matthew 25:31–46)

Matthew 25:31–46 is among the final teachings of Jesus prior to his crucifixion and resurrection. In telling of his return and the final judgment, Jesus described in these verses the kind of faith he is looking for. Nowhere does the Bible indicate that mere mental assent to the existence of God is sufficient for salvation. James 2:19 says, "You believe that God is one. You do well; the demons also believe, and shudder." The kind of faith Jesus requires is the faith that transforms.

The fact that those who were rewarded with eternal life did not know when they had seen him hungry, thirsty, a stranger, naked, sick, or in prison and ministered to him indicates that they were not doing these

WHAT TO DO

- Make a list of those you consider to be the weak and vulnerable in your community. Begin prayerfully to identify ways you can be Christ's hands. Decide what you will do first. Do it.
- Visit the Buckner International website at www.buckner.org, and look for ways you can help care for children at risk in the world.
- Visit the ISAAC website at www.isaacproject.org. Identify ways you and your church can help with immigration needs.
- Consider what your church is doing to participate in disaster relief, and identify ways to be prepared to help when disaster comes.

things to earn their way to heaven. They were simply caring for "the least of these" because that is what the Spirit of God prompted them to do. In the same way, those who were condemned had failed to do these things because their lack of faith left them self-absorbed and callous to those near them who were in need.

Conclusion

We hear constant reports of injustice, abuse, hunger, and victimization in our world. God is concerned about what happens in the streets, the ghettos, and the inner city. He is concerned about what happens to people in need, including the poor, the oppressed, the vulnerable, and the weak of our world. We must be concerned, too.

QUESTIONS

1. What is *your church* doing to care for the weak and vulnerable in your community?

2. What are *you* doing to care for the weak and vulnerable in your community?

3. What resources has God given your church to minister to the weak and vulnerable?

4. Who are the people in your church who work with the weak and vulnerable during the week in their professions? How can you encourage and help them?

NOTES

1. See www.buckner.org.

FOCAL TEXTS
Matthew 28:16–20; Acts 11:19–26; Revelation 5:1–10

BACKGROUND
Matthew 28:16–20; Acts 11:19–26; Revelation 5:1–14

MAIN IDEA
God calls us to participate in his mission to everyone.

QUESTION TO EXPLORE
So are we going to participate in God's mission to everyone or just talk about it?

STUDY AIM
To commit myself to participating in God's mission to everyone

QUICK READ
Jesus has commanded all believers to "make disciples." In the twenty-first century as in the first, God is creating the opportunity to accomplish his purpose so that people of every nation, tribe, and tongue will worship him.

LESSON THIRTEEN
Participate in God's Mission to Everyone

Not long ago I stood at the foot of a lighthouse on the shore of Banda Aceh, Indonesia. The tsunami that hit the coast on December 26, 2004, shattered the windows in the top of this lighthouse.

When I was there, hundreds of Indonesians milled about the rocks and sand, still, it seemed, pondering the devastation that had occurred only a few years earlier. I noticed a woman on a motorcycle. She was watching our American group. Through an interpreter I asked whether I could take her picture. She smiled, agreed, and then told us her story. She was at this place when the tsunami hit. It carried her and her two children two miles inland. Her husband and most of her family were killed. One of her children drowned. Her son was severely injured, and the doctors had given up hope of saving him. But an American doctor, part of the first wave of rescue workers, asked whether he could help. "He saved my son's life," she said. "I want to thank you for coming."

Aceh is the most devout Muslim state in Indonesia. Prior to the tsunami Christians were prevented from entering. Many consider Aceh the doorstep to Mecca, the entry point for Islam into Indonesia, the nation with the largest Muslim population in the world. Most people who live there have never heard of Jesus, except for references to him in the Koran.

I was reminded of haunting questions in the Scripture, "Whom shall I send, and who will go for Us?" (Isaiah 6:8). "How then will they call on Him in whom they have not believed? How will they believe in Him whom they have not heard? And how will they hear without a preacher?" (Romans 10:14). Day after day I watched the Acehnese people going to and from work and school and shopping in the markets. I prayed for them, knowing that almost without exception, they had never heard the gospel.

MATTHEW 28:16–20

¹⁶But the eleven disciples proceeded to Galilee, to the mountain which Jesus had designated. ¹⁷When they saw Him, they worshiped Him; but some were doubtful. ¹⁸And Jesus came up and spoke to them, saying, "All authority has been given to Me in heaven and on earth. ¹⁹"Go therefore and make disciples of all the nations, baptizing them in the name of the Father and the Son and the Holy

Spirit, ²⁰teaching them to observe all that I commanded you; and lo, I am with you always, even to the end of the age."

ACTS 11:19–26

¹⁹So then those who were scattered because of the persecution that occurred in connection with Stephen made their way to Phoenicia and Cyprus and Antioch, speaking the word to no one except to Jews alone. ²⁰But there were some of them, men of Cyprus and Cyrene, who came to Antioch and began speaking to the Greeks also, preaching the Lord Jesus. ²¹And the hand of the Lord was with them, and a large number who believed turned to the Lord. ²²The news about them reached the ears of the church at Jerusalem, and they sent Barnabas off to Antioch. ²³Then when he arrived and witnessed the grace of God, he rejoiced and began to encourage them all with resolute heart to remain true to the Lord; ²⁴for he was a good man, and full of the Holy Spirit and of faith. And considerable numbers were brought to the Lord. ²⁵And he left for Tarsus to look for Saul; ²⁶and when he had found him, he brought him to Antioch. And for an entire year they met with the church and taught considerable numbers; and the disciples were first called Christians in Antioch.

REVELATION 5:1–10

¹I saw in the right hand of Him who sat on the throne a book written inside and on the back, sealed up with seven seals. ²And I saw a strong angel proclaiming with a loud voice, "Who is worthy to open the book and to break its seals?" ³And no one in heaven or on the earth or under the earth was able to open the book or to look into it. ⁴Then I began to weep greatly because no one was found worthy to open the book or to look into it; ⁵and one of the elders said to me, "Stop weeping; behold, the Lion that is from the tribe of Judah, the Root of David, has overcome so as to open the book and its seven seals." ⁶And I saw between the throne (with the four living creatures) and the elders a Lamb standing, as if slain,

> having seven horns and seven eyes, which are the seven Spirits of God, sent out into all the earth. ⁷And He came and took the book out of the right hand of Him who sat on the throne. ⁸When He had taken the book, the four living creatures and the twenty-four elders fell down before the Lamb, each one holding a harp and golden bowls full of incense, which are the prayers of the saints. ⁹And they sang a new song, saying, "Worthy are You to take the book and to break its seals; for You were slain, and purchased for God with Your blood men from every tribe and tongue and people and nation. ¹⁰"You have made them to be a kingdom and priests to our God; and they will reign upon the earth."

The Great Commission (Matthew 28:16–20)

This passage is one of the best-known and most-quoted Scriptures, perhaps second only to John 3:16. It has come to be referred to as the Great Commission. Someone has asked, however, if it would be better named *the Great Suggestion*, since so many Christians pay so little attention to it.

This event occurred during the forty days following Jesus' resurrection. For more than a month Jesus appeared on different occasions in different places to verify that he was raised from the dead (Acts 1:3). On the first day when Jesus was raised from the dead He left instructions for his disciples to meet him in Galilee (Matt. 28:7, 10; Mark 16:7). At least two appearances in Galilee are preserved for us, the appearance on the sea of Tiberias (John 21) and this one on the mountain in Galilee. Afterward the disciples returned to Jerusalem. There Jesus made his final appearance near Bethany before ascending into heaven (Luke 24:49–51).

We often conclude that Jesus commanded us to "go." This is not quite the case. The verb construction translated "go" (Matt. 28:19) actually means *as you go* or *while you are going*. He actually assumed every believer would "go." The command is to "make disciples." This Great Commission of Christ is meant for all believers, not just Christian professionals, *the clergy* and *missionaries.* In the first century there were no professional ministers, and these eleven men were from all walks of life: fishermen, tax collectors, common laborers.

We are to go in our daily experience. If our going is part of Jesus' Great Commission, we ought to consider that where we work, study, and do other daily activities may be, and needs to be, directed by the Holy Spirit. The people with whom we come in contact through our daily activities are people for whom we have responsibility to "make disciples." Wherever we live and work, we can conclude that God has sent us there. When we move to another place, we ought to pray and listen to Jesus' leading.

We are to go on mission trips. Even in the first century, followers of Jesus Christ went on mission trips. Such trips looked different than they do today, but Phillip was on a "mission trip" when he met the Ethiopian treasurer (Acts 8:26–39). Paul, Barnabas, Silas, Timothy, and Luke all went on mission trips and returned to their home church to report on their experience. Every year thousands of believers go on mission trips to countries all over the world. Perhaps the first step each one of us can

THE HELLENISTS

The Hellenists referred to in Acts 11:20 are very significant. Up to this time Greek-speaking Jews had accepted Christ as reflected in Acts 6. Others who were Greek but had converted to Judaism had also accepted Christ. But this is the first time that Greeks who had not become Jews first were coming to Christ. This fact would set up a major crisis for the first-century believers. Could people who were not Jews come to faith in Christ without first becoming Jews by faith? How the church settled this question would ultimately determine whether Christianity was to remain a sect of Judaism or a unique faith standing on its own foundation of faith in Christ alone. The conflict over this issue would result in a personal confrontation between Paul and Peter when Peter visited Antioch (Gal. 2:11). The issue would finally come to a head in Jerusalem following the first missionary journey by Paul and Barnabas (Acts 15). The church leaders affirmed that Gentiles are saved by faith in Christ alone without embracing Judaism (Ephesians 2:8–16).

take toward fulfilling the Great Commission is to get a valid passport so we are ready to go anywhere God calls us to go.

We are to go in our professions. When Paul obeyed Jesus' Great Commission, he took with him his trade as a tent-maker. In Corinth, he lived with Priscilla and Aquila, where he worked making tents in order to share the gospel in the city (Acts 18:3). Today the greatest mission force God is raising up is found among laypeople who are using their professions to make an impact on the world and change it. Some of these use their professions as "tent-makers," making their living in another country or region where they can share the gospel. I met a computer executive in a church where I was speaking who told me his company was outsourcing much of its work to India. I asked him whether he had ever been to India. He said, "No, but if I asked I am sure my company would send me." Many places in Asia offer opportunities for people who can teach English as a second language. Engineers, computer technicians, and chemists are in demand world-wide. In today's global economy followers of Jesus Christ can use their profession to live and witness in many places missionaries cannot go.

We are to "make disciples." Here is the imperative in Jesus' command: "make disciples" (Matt. 28:19). We are all mentors and examples to someone. Someone looks up to you. Jesus demonstrated that making disciples is more than teaching Bible studies. It involves living together so that others can see our actions. Making disciples is more about character and conduct than it is about theology, and becoming a disciple is *caught* more than it is *taught*. This is the reason Jesus said we should teach them to "observe" all he commanded. This is different from teaching them to *know* all he said.

The Great Dispersion (Acts 11:19–26)

Surprisingly, the first-century followers of Jesus did not immediately launch out to carry the gospel to the ends of the earth. Instead, they settled in at Jerusalem. Only after the Jewish authorities launched a severe persecution against the believers in Jerusalem were they "scattered," carrying the good news of Jesus to distant places.

The stoning of Stephen marks the start of this severe persecution (Acts 7). Stephen was one of the seven believers selected to care for the

Greek widows who felt neglected in the daily distribution of food (Acts 6). Like the rest of the seven, he has a Greek name. Stephen is the English transliteration of *stephanos,* which means *wreath* or *crown.*

The Bible is clear that those who were scattered were the laity. Acts 8:1 says, " . . . and they were all scattered throughout the regions of Judaea and Samaria, except the apostles." Average believers began to carry the news of Jesus and the resurrection into places the apostles never thought of going. A spiritual awakening sprang up in Samaria when Philip, another of the seven in Acts 6, shared the gospel there. Samaritans were considered *half-breeds,* and most Jews avoided crossing through Samaria.

Acts 11:19–26 refers to the pivotal experience at Antioch. One of the seven "deacons" listed in Acts 6 is referred to as "Nicolas, a proselyte from Antioch" (6:5). It is quite possible that Nicolas carried the gospel to his home city. For the first time Greeks responded to the gospel, and Bible studies began to spring up all over the city. As a result, the leaders in Jerusalem sent Barnabas to Antioch to verify and encourage God's activity. Barnabas's name means *encouragement,* and his actions were true to his name. He had befriended and encouraged Saul of Tarsus when Saul was a new convert (9:26–27). At Antioch Barnabas encouraged the new Greek converts and sought out Saul to connect him to this remarkable movement of God. God's dispersion of the believers to Antioch launched the mission movement that resulted in the Mediterranean world coming to Christ within three centuries (13:2).

CONNECTING YOUR CHURCH FOR MISSIONS

First Baptist Church, Kaufman, Texas, scheduled a missions weekend with WorldconneX to discover how they could uniquely impact the world with the gospel. They discovered that most of the Hispanics in Kaufman originated from one town in Mexico. First Baptist in Kaufman responded by adopting that city for missions. They are partnering with Kaufman Hispanics and sending teams to reach the city of their origin in Mexico for Christ. How could God connect your church for missions?

God is creating a new dispersion in the twenty-first century, perhaps for a similar purpose. Sometimes people groups are dispersed by war, famine, flood, or disease. Others are dispersed by the global economy. In many cases God is bringing people of other cultures, languages, and races into our communities where we can build relationships with them and introduce them to Jesus Christ.

According to the 2000 census, 2.43 million Chinese live in the United States.[1] The number of Chinese-Americans increased by about 800,000 during the decade of the nineties. The large increase was fueled primarily by an influx of professionals and technology workers as well as relatives of families already living in the United States.

In other cases, God is creating opportunities to disperse us to the ends of the earth in our careers. Not long ago I was in Cairo, Egypt, and had the opportunity to visit with the governor, a graduate of the University of Minnesota. He made it clear that Egypt welcomed and encouraged Americans to create businesses in their country. They need jobs for the many young people graduating every year from their colleges and universities. Many countries—like Egypt, which is about ninety percent Muslim—welcome businesspeople who can help build their economies and create a future for their youth. This creates unique opportunities to build relationships and establish credibility to make disciples in unreached nations.

The Great Conclusion (Revelation 5:1–10)

While exiled on the island of Patmos, John received a vision from God representing the consummation of the age. His vision is filled with imagery and symbolism. Obviously the Lamb represents Jesus Christ, who was "slain and purchased for God with his blood men from every tribe and tongue and people and nation" (Revelation 5:9). Again, the word for "nation" is the Greek word *ethne* (see lesson 11). The references to tribes, tongues, peoples, and nations represents far more than political or geographical boundaries. These are cultural, ethnic, and language groups. From the beginning, the redemption story of God's activity has been about redeeming all peoples of all cultural and ethnic groups. The Book of Psalms, for example, is full of references to God's plan to "disciple the nations" (Psalms 22:27; 57:9; 72:11, 17; 86:9; 108:3; 117:1).

LESSON 13: *Participate in God's Mission to Everyone*

In July 2005 more than 13,000 Baptists from around the world gathered in Birmingham, England, for the 100th anniversary of the Baptist World Alliance. My wife and I were there. What an amazing sight during the procession to see the banners from 113 nations carried into the arena. And what an awesome experience to hear believers singing songs of worship in their native languages! We sensed a small taste of heaven, where a "multitude which no one could count" will worship the Lamb! (Rev. 7:9–10).

Implications and Actions

Almost all—the vast majority—of our communities are changing, and the greatest change is the shift in ethnicity. Anglos now comprise less than fifty percent of the Texas population.[2] What's the situation where you live? In order to share the gospel effectively as God's mission demands, we must find ways to include everyone regardless of ethnicity or cultural identity.

QUESTIONS

1. How can God use you to be a witness for him in your place of work?

2. What do you think it means to be a disciple of Jesus Christ?

3. Do you consider yourself a disciple of Jesus?

4. What different ethnic groups are represented in your church?

5. What responsibility do you feel for sharing the gospel with all people?

6. What do you think of the statements, *It doesn't matter what you believe as long as you believe something?* and *We are all going to the same place anyway?*

NOTES

1. www.census.gov/prod/2004pubs/censr-17.pdf. Accessed 1/26/09.
2. www.dallasfed.org/research/pubs/fotexas/fotexaspetersen.html. Accessed 1/26/09.

Our Next New Study
(Available for use beginning September 2009)

GALATIANS AND THESSALONIANS: Building On a Solid Foundation

GALATIANS: NO OTHER GOSPEL
UNIT ONE. ONLY BY FAITH IN CHRIST JESUS

Lesson 1	Only One Gospel	Galatians 1:1–10
Lesson 2	The Difference the Gospel Makes	Galatians 1:11–24
Lesson 3	United by the Gospel	Galatians 2:1–10
Lesson 4	One Table for God's Church	Galatians 2:11–21
Lesson 5	It's Faith All the Way	Galatians 3:1–18, 26–29
Lesson 6	Set Free to Be God's Children	Galatians 4:1–10; 5:1

UNIT TWO. THE GOSPEL IN LIFE

Lesson 7	Walk by the Spirit	Galatians 5:13–26
Lesson 8	Life in a Good Church	Galatians 6:1–10, 14–16

1 AND 2 THESSALONIANS: GUIDANCE FOR HEALTHY CHURCH LIFE

Lesson 9	Thank God for Such a Church!	1 Thessalonians 1
Lesson 10	The Leadership God Wants	1 Thessalonians 2:1–12
Lesson 11	Live to Please God and Win Others' Respect	1 Thessalonians 4:1–12; 5:14–24
Lesson 12	Hope for Time and Eternity	1 Thessalonians 4:13—5:11
Lesson 13	Being a Thriving Church in a Tough Situation	2 Thessalonians 3:1–16

Additional Resources for Studying Galatians[1]

- Charles B. Cousar. *Galatians*. Interpretation: A Bible Commentary for Teaching and Preaching. Louisville, Kentucky: John Knox Press, 1982.
- Richard B. Hays. "The Letter to the Galatians." *The New Interpreter's Bible*. Volume XI. Nashville, Tennessee: Abingdon Press, 2000.
- Craig S. Keener. *IVP Bible Background Commentary: New Testament*. Downers Grove, Illinois: InterVarsity Press, 1993.
- John William MacGorman. "Galatians." *The Broadman Bible Commentary*. Volume 11. Nashville, Tennessee: Broadman Press, 1971.
- Leon Morris. *Galatians: Paul's Charter of Christian Freedom*. Downers Grove: InterVarsity Press, 1996.
- A.T. Robertson. *Word Pictures in the New Testament*. Volume IV, The Epistles of Paul. Nashville, Tennessee: Broadman Press, 1931.
- Curtis Vaughan. *Galatians: A Study Guide Commentary*. Grand Rapids: Zondervan, 1972.

Additional Resources for Studying 1 and 2 Thessalonians

- F.F. Bruce. *1 & 2 Thessalonians*. Word Biblical Commentary. Volume 45. Waco, Texas: Word Books, Inc., 1982.
- Gary W. Demarest. *1, 2 Thessalonians; 1, 2 Timothy; and Titus*. The Communicator's Commentary. Volume 9. Waco, Texas: Word Books, Inc., 1984.
- Beverly Roberts Gaventa. *First and Second Thessalonians*. Interpretation: A Bible Commentary for Teaching and Preaching. Louisville: John Knox Press, 1998.
- Herschel H. Hobbs. "1—2 Thessalonians." *The Broadman Bible Commentary*. Volume 11. Nashville, Tennessee: Broadman Press, 1971.
- Craig S. Keener. *IVP Bible Background Commentary: New Testament*. Downers Grove, Illinois: InterVarsity Press, 1993.
- Leon Morris. *The First and Second Epistles to the Thessalonians*. The New International Commentary on the New Testament. Grand Rapids, Michigan: Eerdmans, 1959, 1982.
- A.T. Robertson. *Word Pictures in the New Testament*. Volume IV, The Epistles of Paul. Nashville, Tennessee: Broadman Press, 1931.
- Abraham Smith. "The First Letter to the Thessalonians" and "The Second Letter to the Thessalonians." *The New Interpreter's Bible*. Volume XI. Nashville: Abingdon Press, 2000.

Additional Future Adult Bible Studies

The Gospel of Luke: Good News of Great Joy For use beginning December 2009

    (NOTE: This is a special 18-session study that moves through the Gospel of Luke. Classes who begin this study the first Sunday in December will be able to continue the study through Easter.)

Genesis For use beginning April 11, 2010

    (NOTE: This study of Genesis is an 8-session study.)

Living Faith in Daily Life For use beginning June 2010

Letters of James, Peter, and John For use beginning September 2010

NOTES

1. Listing a book does not imply full agreement by the writers or BAPTISTWAY PRESS® with all of its comments.

How to Order More Bible Study Materials

It's easy! Just fill in the following information. For additional Bible study materials, see www.baptistwaypress.org or get a complete order form of available materials by calling 1-866-249-1799 or e-mailing baptistway@bgct.org.

Title of item	Price	Quantity	Cost
This Issue:			
Participating in God's Mission—Study Guide (BWP001077)	$3.55		
Participating in God's Mission—Large Print Study Guide (BWP001078)	$3.95		
Participating in God's Mission—Teaching Guide (BWP001079)	$3.95		
Additional Issues Available:			
Growing Together in Christ—Study Guide (BWP001036)	$3.25		
Growing Together in Christ—Large Print Study Guide (BWP001037)	$3.55		
Growing Together in Christ—Teaching Guide (BWP001038)	$3.75		
Genesis 12—50: Family Matters—Study Guide (BWP000034)	$1.95		
Genesis 12—50: Family Matters—Teaching Guide (BWP000035)	$2.45		
Leviticus, Numbers, Deuteronomy—Study Guide (BWP000053)	$2.35		
Leviticus, Numbers, Deuteronomy—Large Print Study Guide (BWP000052)	$2.35		
Leviticus, Numbers, Deuteronomy—Teaching Guide (BWP000054)	$2.95		
Joshua, Judges—Study Guide (BWP000047)	$2.35		
Joshua, Judges—Large Print Study Guide (BWP000046)	$2.35		
Joshua, Judges—Teaching Guide (BWP000048)	$2.95		
1 and 2 Samuel—Study Guide (BWP000002)	$2.35		
1 and 2 Samuel—Large Print Study Guide (BWP000001)	$2.35		
1 and 2 Samuel—Teaching Guide (BWP000003)	$2.95		
1 and 2 Kings: Leaders and Followers—Study Guide (BWP001025)	$2.95		
1 and 2 Kings: Leaders and Followers Large Print Study Guide (BWP001026)	$3.15		
1 and 2 Kings: Leaders and Followers Teaching Guide (BWP001027)	$3.45		
Ezra, Haggai, Zechariah, Nehemiah, Malachi—Study Guide (BWP001071)	$3.25		
Ezra, Haggai, Zechariah, Nehemiah, Malachi—Large Print Study Guide (BWP001072)	$3.55		
Ezra, Haggai, Zechariah, Nehemiah, Malachi—Teaching Guide (BWP001073)	$3.75		
Job, Ecclesiastes, Habakkuk, Lamentations: Dealing with Hard Times—Study Guide (BWP001016)	$2.75		
Job, Ecclesiastes, Habakkuk, Lamentations: Dealing with Hard Times—Large Print Study Guide (BWP001017)	$2.85		
Job, Ecclesiastes, Habakkuk, Lamentations: Dealing with Hard Times—Teaching Guide (BWP001018)	$3.25		
Psalms and Proverbs: Songs and Sayings of Faith— Study Guide (BWP001000)	$2.75		
Psalms and Proverbs: Songs and Sayings of Faith— Large Print Study Guide (BWP001001)	$2.85		
Psalms and Proverbs: Songs and Sayings of Faith— Teaching Guide (BWP001002)	$3.25		
Matthew: Hope in the Resurrected Christ—Study Guide (BWP001066)	$3.25		
Matthew: Hope in the Resurrected Christ—Large Print Study Guide (BWP001067)	$3.55		
Matthew: Hope in the Resurrected Christ—Teaching Guide (BWP001068)	$3.75		
Mark: Jesus' Works and Words—Study Guide (BWP001022)	$2.95		
Mark: Jesus' Works and Words—Large Print Study Guide (BWP001023)	$3.15		
Mark:Jesus' Works and Words—Teaching Guide (BWP001024)	$3.45		
Jesus in the Gospel of Mark—Study Guide (BWP000066)	$1.95		
Jesus in the Gospel of Mark—Large Print Study Guide (BWP000065)	$1.95		
Jesus in the Gospel of Mark—Teaching Guide (BWP000067)	$2.45		
Luke: Journeying to the Cross—Study Guide (BWP000057)	$2.35		
Luke: Journeying to the Cross—Large Print Study Guide (BWP000056)	$2.35		
Luke: Journeying to the Cross—Teaching Guide (BWP000058)	$2.95		
The Gospel of John: The Word Became Flesh—Study Guide (BWP001008)	$2.75		
The Gospel of John: The Word Became Flesh—Large Print Study Guide (BWP001009)	$2.85		
The Gospel of John: The Word Became Flesh—Teaching Guide (BWP001010)	$3.25		
Acts: Toward Being a Missional Church—Study Guide (BWP001013)	$2.75		
Acts: Toward Being a Missional Church—Large Print Study Guide (BWP001014)	$2.85		
Acts: Toward Being a Missional Church—Teaching Guide (BWP001015)	$3.25		
Romans: What God Is Up To—Study Guide (BWP001019)	$2.95		
Romans: What God Is Up To—Large Print Study Guide (BWP001020)	$3.15		
Romans: What God Is Up To—Teaching Guide (BWP001021)	$3.45		

Ephesians, Philippians, Colossians—Study Guide (BWP001060)	$3.25
Ephesians, Philippians, Colossians—Large Print Study Guide (BWP001061)	$3.55
Ephesians, Philippians, Colossians—Teaching Guide (BWP001062)	$3.75
1, 2 Timothy, Titus, Philemon—Study Guide (BWP000092)	$2.75
1, 2 Timothy, Titus, Philemon—Large Print Study Guide (BWP000091)	$2.85
1, 2 Timothy, Titus, Philemon—Teaching Guide (BWP000093)	$3.25
Revelation—Study Guide (BWP000084)	$2.35
Revelation—Large Print Study Guide (BWP000083)	$2.35
Revelation—Teaching Guide (BWP000085)	$2.95

Coming for use beginning September 2009

Galatians and 1&2 Thessalonians—Study Guide (BWP001080)	$3.55
Galatians and 1&2 Thessalonians—Large Print Study Guide (BWP001081)	$3.95
Galatians and 1&2 Thessalonians—Teaching Guide (BWP001082)	$3.95

Standard (UPS/Mail) Shipping Charges*			
Order Value	Shipping charge**	Order Value	Shipping charge**
$.01—$9.99	$6.50	$160.00—$199.99	$22.00
$10.00—$19.99	$8.00	$200.00—$249.99	$26.00
$20.00—$39.99	$9.00	$250.00—$299.99	$28.00
$40.00—$59.99	$10.00	$300.00—$349.99	$32.00
$60.00—$79.99	$11.00	$350.00—$399.99	$40.00
$80.00—$99.99	$12.00	$400.00—$499.99	$48.00
$100.00—$129.99	$14.00	$500.00—$599.99	$58.00
$130.00—$159.99	$18.00	$600.00—$799.99	$70.00**

Cost of items (Order value) _____

Shipping charges (see chart*) _____

TOTAL _____

*Plus, applicable taxes for individuals and other taxable entities (not churches) within Texas will be added. Please call 1-866-249-1799 if the exact amount is needed prior to ordering.

**For order values $800.00 and above, please call 1-866-249-1799 or check www.baptistwaypress.org

Please allow three weeks for standard delivery. For express shipping service: Call 1-866-249-1799 for information on additional charges.

YOUR NAME _____ PHONE _____

YOUR CHURCH _____ DATE ORDERED _____

SHIPPING ADDRESS _____

CITY _____ STATE _____ ZIP CODE _____

E-MAIL _____

MAIL this form with your check for the total amount to
BAPTISTWAY PRESS, Baptist General Convention of Texas,
333 North Washington, Dallas, TX 75246-1798
(Make checks to "Baptist Executive Board.")

OR, **FAX** your order anytime to: 214-828-5376, and we will bill you.

OR, **CALL** your order toll-free: 1-866-249-1799
(M-Th 8:30 a.m.-6:00 p.m.; Fri 8:30 a.m.-5:00 p.m. central time),
and we will bill you.

OR, **E-MAIL** your order to our internet e-mail address:
baptistway@bgct.org, and we will bill you.

OR, **ORDER ONLINE** at www.baptistwaypress.org.

We look forward to receiving your order! Thank you!